<u>How to Rewire Your Brain</u>

Change Your Mind and Habits. Better Rules and Positive Thinking to Improve Your Life. Stop Worrying and Increase Your Power to Influence People

David Michael King

information. No warranties of any kind are declared or implied. Readers acknowledge that the author is not engaging in the rendering of legal, financial, medical or professional advice. The content within this book has been derived from various sources. Please consult a licensed professional before attempting any techniques outlined in this book. By reading this document, the reader agrees that under no circumstances is the author responsible for any losses, direct or indirect, which are incurred as a result of the use of information contained within this document, including, but not limited to, errors, omissions, or inaccuracies.

Table of Contents

Introduction: When the Mind/Brain Becomes Overwhelming

From the moment we are born, we begin to feel the effects of the environment. From then on, we are alive, and our personalities begin to form in union with that environment. The Nature vs. Nurture argument proceeds instantaneously; parents start worrying about whether or not their skills are going to entirely shape the personality of their child, whether the punishment will turn them into a serial killer, or the lack of it will make them stand up citizens in society. How they are spoken to, their patterned responses, the amount of affection they give to the child, can be obsessively watched and innately criticized by the parents or those around them.

The nature of personality has also been heavily studied within the field of psychology, ranging from the late 1800s to even advancements in the early 2000s. What makes a person is a cluster of several characteristics that are forged from several aspects of genetics, as well as the distinct influence from the environment in which they are raised. Important occurrences can shape a person's knee jerk responses to later stimuli, where sensitivity to the initial occurrence could have been something that was genetically inevitable. As we grow older, obligations, expectations, and necessities of life grow larger and feel much heavier. Eventually, once a person has left school, they try to begin forming the path to their own independent life. Also, depending upon what kind of environment they were raised in, the concept of going off on their own may be foreign or not an option at all.

Many children are raised in homes where the expectations of the parents are put onto them, such as caring for a sibling or having to obtain work at an early age. Extreme personality shaping experiences such as abuse and observation of addiction place the child in an environment that is consistently anxiety-provoking, so much to the point where they grow into adults who are unable to emotionally, financially and physically manage themselves. Others feel the burden of paying bills, paying for school, dealing with different kinds of parental, familial, romantic and platonic relationships, the struggle of constructing a self-identity, and the list goes on and on. This weight is something that all human beings experience, and it is called stress.

Stress, on a practical level, is the experience of the hormone cortisol. This hormone is responsible for many other regulations in the body but has mainly been demonized for its relationship with how humans experience stress. Stress is sometimes necessary, as are all basic human emotions.

Evolution has taught us that stress is the experience of the flight or fight response; a reactionary occurrence in the body that releases cortisol, causing several physiological reactions, such as the tensing of the abdomen, the experience of gastrointestinal issues, rapid heart rate, and shortness of breath. What this physiologically indicates to humans is that we are in danger and that we must decide whether or not we are going to 'fight' (or deal with or problem solve) this apparent stimulus, or flee from it (escape it). Initially, this would reference threats from predators, or other physically threatening issues. Now, we can feel it when we are standing in line for coffee, and are worried that we are going to be late for work.

We may still feel it if we are deciding how to defend ourselves when being held at gunpoint (at actual physical threat) but the experience of the stress in the coffee line is a much more modern take on what was initially meant to help keep us safe.

This is an evolved reaction, that can sometimes still be somewhat helpful, but when overly experienced, it can morph into something far more debilitating than a single moment of worry. It is not surprising in this constant stop-and-go society that there are many people who are experiencing the prolonged sensations of stress.

The balancing of work and relationships is a simple example; you want to make enough money so you can support yourself, or possibly a family as well, but the hikes in property tax, goods, and services, transportation, medical bills, etc., continue to spike. You would like to be able to relax and spend time with those you care about, but all you can think about is how that time is not being used to make more money. Perhaps you have lost the feeling of a healthy balance, or even, haven't ever understood what a balance truly looks like.

The scope of every person's life is going to vary, basing itself on several key factors. But no matter what your factors look like, it is highly likely that you are suffering from a general sense of discontentment in your life. Perhaps there is more to life than a job and career goals to you. Perhaps you are constantly tired and are unable to formulate a successful schedule that allows engaging in everything you want to in a day. Maybe your emotions run you, as opposed to you running your own emotions. Your brain may be feeling like it is tangled and flipped upside down, and you have no idea where you can start.

Fortunately for you, there are many people in this situation. Those people are who this book is going to speak directly to; the lost, the confused, the unorganized, the engagers of bad habits, the overly emotional. The human brain is an incredible organ, and unlike other parts of the body that are unable to heal themselves, has proven to be magnificently receptive to change.

This book is going to show you how you can instill new habits, methods of organization, emotion control, and the management of some mental health disorders that have developed from the constant exposure to consistent intense levels of stress. It is never too late to try to turn your life around, to rewire those neurological pathways of your brain, and to finally live a life that is full of promise, joy, relaxation, and achievement.

Chapter 1: Common Habits and Behaviors of Mentally Unhappy and Unhealthy People

The range of what is categorized as unhappy and unhealthy varies widely. A good general description to refer to is a consistent lack of contentment. What is contentment, you ask? Contentment is a general sensation of ease, comfort, happiness, while also experiencing the lack of prolonged sensations of unhappiness, lack of motivation, and stress. This book is not going to solve all of your problems and turn you into someone who is never unhappy. Humans are still meant to feel stress, sadness, disappointment, anger, but in a healthy, less intense and less prolonged manner. You will find that the main difference between people who are mentally unhappy and unhealthy and those are the opposite, is how the people who are mentally happy and healthy cope with the experience of internal emotions as well as external events.

This chapter is going to explore the aspects of several habits and behaviors of those people who identify themselves as being mentally unhappy and unhealthy.

This is the part of the book where you can try to identify certain habits that you feel you engage in. If none of them are coming to mind, try to give yourself a week of observation. Read over this chapter, and try to notice when you are partaking in one or more of the behaviors listed in this section. Get a notebook or something that is small and handy that you can carry wherever you go. At this point, do your best not to judge yourself; this is merely the observation phase. The phase of change will come later in this book. If you are able to specifically identify certain behaviors, word them specifically in relation to this book. You can come back to your notebook for later reference once your progress in your reading.

We will divide up these habits into two sections; the ones that are psychological in nature and the other that are behavioral in nature. One may affect the other, but it will become easier to notice how each bad habit interlinks with another once you begin observing yourself.

1.1 Unhealthy Psychological Habits

- Self-Criticism: There is a big difference between healthy self-criticism and unhealthy self-criticism. This is particularly damaging when your self-esteem is already at an all-time low. This can manifest itself either internal (through negative self-talk) or externally (through self-deprecating jokes, underestimating yourself). When something bad happens to you externally, such as missing a job promotion, not getting a call back from that person you went on a date with, you may respond with self-talk that is harsh, unkind, and even abusive.

This is rationalized within us because some of us may believe that we deserve being spoken to this way. We also do this so we can prepare ourselves to be disappointed again. This is a faulty habit. The next time something happens that is disappointing, our habit of self-abuse has been so reinforced that it will quickly rise to the occasion once a perceived failure comes to fruition. We also may be engaging in something within psychology that is called a 'self-fulfilling prophecy'. What this states, in essence, are that if we expect ourselves to fail, we are going to put minimal effort into achieving the goal, and therefore when we do fail, we are not surprised. This does not nurture the notion of confidence or the concept of a positive outlook, which makes it harder to face our fears and achieve goals.

- "Psyching" Ourselves out after a Failure: It is a commonly mistaken human habit to convince ourselves after we've failed at something that the goal was impossible in the first place. This, of course, means that we are not going to try for it again, or at least, allow a decrease in effort and motivation toward achieving it. We sometimes tell ourselves that we are trying to be more realistic, so we are not disappointed in the future. Again, this is not healthy because what we are actually doing to ourselves is giving into your perception distortions as opposed to using the failure as a lesson that can teach how to behave more sues fully in the future.

- Pushing People Away: Ironically, when people are lonelier, they are more likely to push others away. People develop this habit because of experiences of the past that have made them feel emotionally hurt and insecure. We convince ourselves that avoiding connections is the way to go; if you aren't close to someone, then you cannot get hurt. All this does is push away any of the potential people in our lives who we may have had a chance to get close to, and possibly improve our level of contentment in our lives.

- Indulging in the Urge to Brood and Ruminate: People who suffer from clinical depression, anxiety, and even physical health problems, all tend to be individuals who ruminate over negatively perceived incidents in their lives. It is entirely normal and natural to assess what may have gone wrong in an interaction, an event, a relationship, or even a job performance in order to learn about what we can do better next time. But when we ruminate constantly upon the same issues, event, interactions, our brains can get stuck on a loop. No solution is reached, and only the problems of the interaction or event are looked at and criticized from every angle. We tell ourselves that we are processing our emotions, but we are actually merely engaging in demoralization ourselves. This is a highly inactive approach to problem-solving that can lead to several mental health issues that will be discussed later on.

- Distancing Ourselves When We Feel Guilty Instead of Repairing the Relationship: Guilt occurs when we do or say something that could either intentionally or unintentionally hurt another person. Many people do their best to avoid apologizing or engaging in behaviors that could help resolve the issue, such as reaching out to them. The tension only lingers, and the relationship receives more and more damage. We rationalize this behavior by telling ourselves we have already apologized, and that the rest of the resolution lies within the hands of the other person. Apologies are fruitless when it lacks a statement of empathy that recognizes how our actions affected the other person, from their perspective.

- Assuming a Negative Bias: A person who has engaged in looking at life from a negative perspective is generally going to continue to do so unless something so severe disrupts this pattern. This may have something to do with your childhood or even the way that your parents or caregivers think. People with a more negative bias expect that the worst is always going to happen. An extreme version of this is the experience and diagnosis of anxiety and depressive disorders. They may believe that the plane they are taking is going to crash, or when sitting down for a job interview, that they are not going to get the job. This way of thinking drains the color out of life and internally causes us to never try any harder for what we want out of life.

- Possess an External Locus of Control: People who engage in this unhealthy way of thinking believe that everything that happens to them is fate. Many people continuously believe that they have bad luck, that their life is just simply bad, and that they have no control over what is happening to them in their lives. As a result of this, they take very little responsibility, if any, for what happens to them, and tend to blame others for the negative occurrences in life.

- Searching for the Easy Way Out: People who think in an unhealthy manner always want things to be quick and easy. They want there to be immediate results, at the exact moment that they want them to be. They want change to happen instantly, which of course leads to constant disappointment when it doesn't. This is also why when trying to change bad habits, these people often give up, because change isn't in that exact time in their life when they want it.

- Lack of Goals: A lot of unhealthy people would like things to be better in their lives, but they are no goals set or plans made that are going to help them achieve this. People with these issues often flail around in life, not truly knowing what they want, afraid to make goals because they are not sure they can achieve them.

- Jealous of Others Success: Some people with unhealthy thinking habits feel jealous of those who have things they do not. This can exist monetarily, thrive by feeling envy toward another's attractiveness or relationship status, or even the ability to create their own new habits. They cannot recognize the hard work that the person has put in order to receive the reward, they merely brood upon the fact that they do not have them.

- Not Listening to Knowledgeable Experts: A lot of people with unhealthy habits ignore the advice of people who are experts in their field, such as doctors, dentists, therapists, or financial advisors. This is done because they do not want to take responsibility for their behavior.

- Avoid Creative-Problem Solving: Not only do these individuals avoid problem-solving altogether, usually, but they also tend to have a one-track mind when it comes to their own version of solving an issue. They often remain stuck because they can only summon a single idea about how to solve a problem. They do not want to engage in creative thinking because this means that their way, may not be the correct way after all.

- Constant Gossiping: These individuals focus on judging others rather than trying to improve their own lives. It is easier to focus on another person's problem rather than your own because you are not the one being internally affected by it.

The following list will discuss common thinking habits that those who have mental health disorders such as obsessive-compulsive disorder, generalized anxiety disorder, social phobia, and levels of depressive disorders tend to engage in. Those who are on the edge of developing these disorders may also engage in thinking unhealthy ways of thinking:

1.2 Cognitive Distortions

Cognitive distortions are described as inaccurate thoughts that reinforce negative thought patterns or emotions. They are faulty ways of thinking that convince the person of a reality that simply is not true. These are patterns of thinking that have been practiced for the majority of our lives, and thus make it more ingrained into our perception of reality.

CBT seeks to address and restructure the process of thinking that involves these cognitive disruptions. First, the most common cognitive distortions will be listed and described. Later, in the section that particularly explores the experience of mental health issues, exercises will be introduced that can help you identify your most applied cognitive distortions, and how you can challenge them.

- Filtering: This refers to the tendency to only see the negative aspect of things throughout our day, our life, or a particular situation. For example, you may have been stuck in traffic, but you still managed to arrive on time for your event and had a good time. Some people who apply to filter may dwell on the fact that they were/are stuck in traffic and how much it distrusts their mood.

- Polarized thinking ("Black and White" Thinking): This is the tendency to look at situations in two extreme ways; everything is either very bad or very good. There is nothing of a mixture in the middle. Either you had a great time at the party, or it was horrible.

- Overgeneralization: This is when a person can take an incident and use it as the sole pieces of evidence that arrives upon a much broader conclusion. For example, a person may have been dating around, had one bad date, and concluded that they will never find a partner in life-based merely upon the experience of this one date.

- Jumping to conclusions: This is the act of feeling sure of something without evidence at all. This distortion can thrive within anxiety and depression, as the tendency to believe in imagined outcomes is natural to the disorder. An anxious person may believe that they may get hit by a car crossing the street, or a depressed person may believe that they have no future at all.

- Personalization: The belief that everything an individual does has a direct impact on external events or other people. The link is usually irrational. For example, a person with anxiety might believe that because they forgot to bring food to a party that everyone will not enjoy the party, because of their mistake.

- Control Fallacies: This is the belief that everything that happens to us is either entirely our fault or entirely caused by forces outside of our control. What occurs in life is generally a combination of both? An example of this is believing that our work performance is because of our managers, or that mistakes made by others are caused by the mistakes we made.

- The fallacy of Fairness: This is an extreme take what is deemed 'fair' in life. The person believes that because they are a good person, or have done good things in life, they deserve to live a life that is fair. This is simply not the case as life goes on.

- Blaming: When things do not go well, or we are not feeling right, a person who practices this cognitive distortion will look outward and blame others for how they act and what they are feeling.

- Shoulds: This distortion refers to the unspoken or spoken rules of how we believe in our culture or society should behave. When others break the rules, we are hurt, when we break our rules, we feel shame and guilt. This leads to unrealistic expectations of ourselves or others that are all mental rather than existing in reality. For example, we may feel guilty if we spend too much money on ourselves if we think overspending isn't okay. We may become angry at a waiter or waitress if we believe they 'should' be constantly filling up our water glass, but isn't.

- Emotional Reasoning: This is the belief that if we feel a certain way, then it must be a true fact. For example, if we feel like something we said made us sound stupid, then we must indeed be stupid in reality. This is an incredibly common distortion that immediately connects emotions to facts. This is an important distortion to note before approaching the cognitive restructuring section of this chapter.

- The fallacy of Change: This is the expectation that others should change in order to suit our needs. This connects to the feeling that our happiness depends highly on other people. This is a very unhealthy way to live because we cannot control others, and making them responsible for our happiness is simply not anyone else's duty but our own.

- Global Labelling/Mislabelling: This is an extreme form of generalizing; this is where we take small instances of evidence and apply it on a global scale. You may have tried to learn to drive a few times in your life but conclude that you will never be able to drive due to these few experiences. It is exaggerated judgments based on the single occurrence, such as a person saying something slightly rude, and concluding that they are an overall bad person.

- Always being Right: This distortion makes us believe that we must always be right in order to be happy. Some people have believed that being happy is more important than being kind to others, and have a difficult time admitting when they have made a mistake.

- Heaven's Reward Fallacy: This involves the false belief that any act of self-sacrifice we commit will pay off. Some may call this karma and will believe that there exists an immediate award, whether tangibly or in praise. This leaves a person bitter when they do not receive the reward that they are expecting.

- Catastrophizing/Magnifying or Minimizing: This involves the expectation that the worst will always happen, or has already happened. This evidence will be based on the smallest incident that is much smaller than the person interprets it as. If you make a mistake at work, there exists a fear that you will get fired because of it. Minimizing is when a person does not focus on a positive occurrence in their life and downplays it to uncontrollable external forces rather than their own dedication or hard work.

1.3 Unhealthy Behavioral Habits

The following are the list of the behaviors that may connect to the way those who are unhealthy think. Behavior and thought patterns work in tandem, each motivating and reinforcing the presence of the other. So do not worry if it is still difficult to identify some of your own unhealthy habits.

- A Bad Sleep Routine: You may not have a very good routine set around sleeping or even a routine at all. Maybe you stay up late some nights, sleep in late some days, to do the point where your energy is all over the place. You may get enough sleep, but choose to stay up late, either working or binging on your favorite TV show. Although there is nothing wrong with doing this every now and then, doing it on a consistent basis may encourage more negative thought patterns. A higher percentage of negative thoughts arrive at night, forcing you to become more and more overwhelmed by their presence. Staying up late may also mean that you are less energetic the next day, and thus, less productive.

- Not Taking Time to Relax: It may be due to work, relationships, kids, etc. Whatever is taking u most of your time and causing you to stress is more than likely going to affect your mental and physical health if you do not take the time to take it easy. Depending upon whether you have a mental health disorder and other internal and external stressors in your life, the way that you need to relax may vary. But no matter who you are, everyone needs time to themselves to feel calm without distractions. If you don't do this, then you are definitely going to feel/be unhealthy, and more likely to engage in other unhealthy behaviors and thinking patterns.

- Lacking Physical Activity: It has been proven through decades of research about depression and other mental health issues that physical activity acts as a great mood booster. When you are moving ore and exercising, more blood moves through your body, shaking out the tension you may be feeling, as well as stimulating neurochemicals dopamine and serotonin that have a direct link to a positive mood.

- Spending a Lot of Time with Toxic People: If you want to improve your life and habits, one of the obstacles to your self-improvement may lie within the confines of who you choose to surround yourself with. If you are with people who put you down, undermined your skill and success, do not respect your boundaries, then it is likely that you too are going to be like this.

- Excessive Use of Technology: Using our computers, phones, and other electronic devices is a way of life for most people in this century. They can help us be more efficient, but they can also act as a distraction, aiding us in avoiding ways that can help our lives improve. Social media accounts give the brain a lot of stimulation, which means that it is harder to calm yourself down after finally turning the computer or phone off.

- Avoiding Your Emotions: You may try to avoid what you are feeling in order to abolish the intense sensation of it. Instead of learning to deal with them, you suppress them. You try to distract yourself, you change the subject, you lie when those in your life ask you how you are. You may drink excessively, eat excessively, gamble, spend, etc., in order to keep those emotions from rising up to ahead. But it has been proven psychologically that we have to somehow process our emotions in a healthy way. When we bury them, they become harder to identify, and thus, harder to successfully face and treat.

- Perfectionism: It is important to try to do your best at something in life, especially when that thing is important to you. The desire to do something flawlessly may increase your chances of actually reaching your goals. But if you feel that you must be perfect at everything, then you are going to fall into the trap of being a perfectionist.

Being a perfectionist isn't as good as it sounds. There are ways that being a perfectionist t can leak out of being a positive enhancement to your character, to acting as a detractor. If you expect yourself to be perfect at everything, then you are going to at some point, feel like you are letting yourself down. People can have a variety of skills, but no one is perfect at everything. You set standards for yourself that are not realistic, and you are not satisfied with any form of achievement unless it is completely flawless. It is likely that you will fall off the deep end with depression and anxiety if you continue to judge yourself harshly for making even the smallest of mistakes.

- Constant Guilt: The feeling of guilt can be pervasive in one's life, even in ways that are subconscious to them. It can manifest itself in children through guilt put onto children from parents, and grow into guilt felt when going to work, and guilt when leaving work. If you perpetually feel guilty about something that is misappropriated to an event, then you are unable to give your entire attention to a single task. Habits that involve guilt include the desire to solve problems that are not our own, self-blaming, perceiving yourself as a bad person for doing something minor, and the inability to forgive yourself.

- Constant Regret: Everyone has felt regret at some point in their life. That is entirely normal. But like the majority of symptoms that fall under the category of unhealthy, they are average behaviors and thinking patterns that grow into constant, unadaptable ones.

The sensation of regret can manifest itself through rumination, which can lead and connect to the feelings involved in depression. Constantly assessing what could have been, pin you to the past, while the only place that you can learn to thrive is in the present.

- Co-dependency: This habit intrudes on your ability to enjoy a healthy and satisfying relationship. This is when a person depends too heavily on another, whether it be romantically, parent-child, platonic, that the relationship becomes unhealthy. It is generally when it is a one-sided relationship, where the sufferer puts themselves constantly ahead of others, even if that means damaging their own mental or physical health. A real relationship relies on a balance, not a single person doing the entire care-taking.

- Ignoring Clutter: If you have certain corners of your home or apartment where you are storing things, it may be acting as a subtle source of psychological stress. By not dealing with it, we are simply avoiding our problems, rather than dealing with them.

- Bottling Up Anger: It happens to be the case that with all human emotions, bottling them up is the worst route to take. Emotions left unprocessed are more likely to turn into other, more serious mental health disorders down the line. Feeling angry, again, is normal, but you must find healthy ways to express that anger so it doesn't grow inside of you.

- Working too much: Yes, there is such a thing as working too much. A lack of balance means that you are not taking the time to relax and not feel the pressure that comes with daily work. This means that you are simply building up with stress, and you are less likely to actually be productive in your day-to-day work.

- Procrastination: Every person at some point in their lives has put a task off to another time, whether it be work, familial, or mundane related. We may put off taking out the trash or doing the dishes, or we may be putting off making an appointment to go to the dentist for that toothache we've been suffering with. No matter how big or small the activity fairs in your life, procrastination is a habit that is learned, and one of the hardest to break. Of course, doing everything you need to do all at once is not realistic, and can also drain you of the appropriate energy required for everyday functioning. But if you find that you are putting off everything in your life, especially the more vital things, you are simply delaying something that you are eventually going to have to deal with anyway. The dishes will stack up, the trash won't take itself out, and your toothache won't go away through avoidance and passive thinking.

- Pessimism: This is another fancy word for giving in to a negative bias. Looking at the world and events within in through a negative mindset is only going to allow your negative situations and negative interpretations of events. It is common with people who are suffering from debilitating depression and/or anxiety to look at even the most positive of events in life through a negative lens. For example, if they get a promotion, or even find money on the ground, they will find a way to see it in a negative light. This is because the road to negativity has been traveled on far too many times, and the brains neurological systems know the way all too well.

- Staying in Your Comfort Zone: You don't have to suffer from a mental health disorder to engage in this incredibly toxic habit. We all have areas in our lives where we feel most comfortable to be ourselves; whether it be working from home, working within a certain industry, only engaging in activities that we know we are good at, etc. But being unwilling to try something new will leave us in the same place in our lives; sitting idle, unchallenged, comfortable and seemingly content, but not growing. Many people do not step outside their comfort zone because they don't know how to deal with the various emotions that come with it, such as anxiety and fear. The fear of failure is a very strong motivator for many people too. But if you don't try, you truly will never know; you could miss out on a new person, a new skill, a new interest, a new career.

- Not Setting Boundaries: The inability to set boundaries or to follow them is a habit that is developed during childhood. Certain caregivers and parents may have their own versions of what it means to have boundaries or even none at all. Some children will grow up to allow people to take advantage of them because they see themselves as 'nice' and don't want to break that positive image. But in reality, setting boundaries for yourself is entirely healthy. Setting boundaries for others means that you learn to be more assertive, you learn to say no, and you feel less guilt when voicing what it is that you want and need. This will be harder the older you are, and the less instilled boundaries that may exist within your family or friend group. But everyone is capable of learning, no matter your age or life stage.

- Bad Eating Habits: A lot of people who are busy working, do not take the time to eat either enough or the right kinds of food. This book is not going to dive too deep into the notion of diets, as they are entirely dependent upon each person and what their goals are through that diet. But eating does play an important role in health and lack of happiness. Our rushed world seems to accept the idea of eating just a single bagel with cream cheese in the morning, pumping down liters of caffeine throughout the day, only to crash in the evening with possibly a nibble of a granola bar in our stomach. This isn't good for our mental and physical health, because we are not getting enough energy and nutrients to aid in our growth and maintenance.

- Not Exercising: It has proven over decades of research that exercise is paramount in order to live a healthy and contently life. You don't have to be at the gym 24/7 or sculpt a six-pack of abs in order to be deemed healthy. Once more, it depends upon your genetics, your body shape/type, your eating habits, as well as your fitness goals, as to how much exercise will benefit your mental and physical health. There is a general consensus though, that at least half an hour, five days a week, will have that dopamine and serotonin pumping enough through your brain to keep you coming back for more.

Most of what will be spoken about in this book is going to be new habits and strategies to instill in your daily living, that are meant to abandon these old ways of behaving and thinking. Take another look at your notebook, and re-read the various habits that you feel you have become caught in as of late. If you are not feeling happy or content, then there is a definite reason for that. What you have been doing so far for yourself isn't working, so why not step out of that comfort zone, and try something new?

Chapter 2: Common Behaviors and Traits of Happy and Healthy People

This chapter is going to look at individuals who have managed to infuse positive and healthy habits into their lives. Once you have finished your list of habits that you feel are the most intrusive in your life, make a hierarchy of 5-10 (depending how many habits you are concerned about), with the higher number as your first and least worrisome, the smaller number, the most worrisome. Once you have done that, take a read over this chapter. You may have tried a couple of them at some point in your life, or maybe you already do it, but in a less consistent manner. Write down these positive habits that you want to try that will counteract your negative ones. Again, do your best not to judge yourself; changing long-term habits takes time, courage, and dedication. It is all a process.

- Be Busy, but Not Rushed: There is a difference between being positively busy and negatively busy. A person, who is constantly working, at work or at home, or even both, is probably rushed, charged by caffeine and deadlines to meet. Generally, those that feel rushed are a person taking on everything that is offered to them, especially when it comes to working. We feel that we need to do everything in order to keep the high-ups satisfied, even things that push the limits of our mental and physical health. This leaves us drained, and unable to focus on the things that we actually might enjoy, should they not be lost in the shuffle of obligations. Healthy and happy people choose the activities that they feel they can achieve, so they can focus on them, rather than worrying about everything else that they have to finish by a certain deadline. This allows them to work at a comfortable pace, which leaves them feeling productive and not miserable at the end of the day or week. The habits that they have instilled are one where they've learned to say no to things that would overwhelm them, and say yes to the right things that will help them feel more productive.

- Have Five Close Relationships: People who suffer from low self-esteem tend to think that they have the more friends you have, the happier you are. In reality, these people are probably trying to fill a void that makes them feel likable. But the number 5 seems to be the most common number within research on relationships and its link to our happiness. Sharing important emotions, memories and intimacies with those around us help us to feel heard, connected, and understood. If we are able to do that with a small number of people, then they are more likely to thrive than trying to balance an excess of people whose interactions with dissolve over time. Relationships are maintained through exchanges of emotions and information, with equal effort from both sides constantly being made.

- Creating and Maintaining Boundaries: As previously mentioned, it can be very difficult to create boundaries with friends and family if you haven't done so in the past. It may seem abrupt to people in your life that are used to being able to cross the line on a consistent basis. But healthy and happy people have learned to create and maintain the boundaries they put into place so they can continue to thrive in a more flourishing environment. This doesn't mean that you have to completely cut someone off. It just means that you are learning to take care of yourself, and constantly being around people that drain you of your optimism and joy isn't good for your mental health. Steps on how to do this will be explored in the next chapter.

- Don't Tie Your Happiness to External Events: It is incredibly common for most people to tie how they feel about themselves and their lives to events that are temporary in nature. People tie it to how much money they make, what their grades are like in school, their status in a certain friend group, etc. One's self-esteem can receive a boost when something external like this occurs, but it is a minute and fickle boost, capable of dropping easily once the next negatively interrupting event occurs. Happy and healthy people do not value their identity based on these shallow components of their lives. They lean more on how kind they are to people, their interests and joys felt within the scope of their hobbies, and achievements that lie within confidence and spiritual development and not the external world.

- Becoming Assertive: There is a great difference between being assertive and being aggressive. Many people tend to link the two together. But they could not be any more different. A person who tries to be assertive may feel like they are being too aggressive, so they do not try to voice their opinion or something that they may want or need. Being aggressive means you demand something for yourself unkindly, while being assertive means you are able to articulate exactly what it is that you need from someone in a polite and direct manner. This skill is greatly connected with creating boundaries, as you need to learn to be more assertive when trying to set up new and clear boundaries for those in your life who don't know how to respect them. This skill will also be explored in the next chapter.

- Exercising Consistently: There is just no way around this. Everyone is going to benefit from physical activity, one way or another. The release of endorphins has been proven to greatly help your mood, and the benefit to your physical health is unrelenting. Healthy and happy people, even if they don't like exercising, find something that falls under one of their interests, and makes it a habit to exercise a handful of times a week.

- Embracing Discomfort: This goes along with the idea of breaking out of your comfort zone. Doing this consistently will help it become a habit, rather than giving in to the desire to hide away from what makes us uncomfortable. Happy people have learned that just because you feel uncomfortable doing something new, doesn't mean that the experience in itself is 'bad'. Struggling through something, a new hobby or skill, is the first step taken to master something. Going out into public and engaging in socially anxious situations will by virtue of science, help you to feel less anxious as time goes on. If you are willing to try anything new, and no longer fear not being good at it, then the world will open up to you.

- Do Not Ignore Your Dreams: One of the main regrets of people who are on their deathbeds is that they did not follow their dreams. The Guardian asked a hospice nurse, who came up with the Top 5 Regrets of the Dying:

"This was the most common regret of all. When people realize that their life is almost over and look back clearly on it, it is easy to see how many dreams have gone unfulfilled. Most people had not honored even a half of their dreams and had to die knowing that it was due to choices they had made, or not made. Health brings a freedom very few realize until they no longer have it."

A dream can be anything as small as learning to paint or wanting to open up your own bar. There are always practical elements in life to consider, but there is a way to achieve any goal as well. All it takes is determination, organization, and patience (which will also be explored later in this book).

- Staying Proactive: Being a proactive person means that you look at problems directly in the face, and choose to solve them constructively, rather than complaining about them and avoiding them. Being proactive is particularly important in romantic relationships, as they are likely to be challenged the longer a relationship is maintained. Problems are going to arise in life no matter what, but it is how we choose to face them and handle them that will affect the emotional and practical result.

- View Problems as Challenges, Rather Than Problems: This connects directly with the mention of problem-solving above. As mentioned, no one lives a life that is empty entirely of challenges or issues. But sometimes our inner dialogue is so obsessed with locating 'problems' in our lives that we are unable to notice how this challenge can actually work to benefit us in the end. Eliminating the word 'problem' from your dialogue and mental dialogue is the first step in re-categorizing the interpretation of external events. A challenge such as realizing that you have gained more weight than you wanted will help you learn to alter your nutritional and exercising habits for the better. A stiff neck can challenge you to recognize that you do need to call the doctor sooner rather than later.

- Rewarding Yourself: Learning to form new habits can be draining. Life, in general, can also be draining. If you feel you have been working hard, try rewarding yourself with a night-in, some red wine, or playing video games, can both help to boost your mood, and to help condition you to keep trying toward maintaining those positive habits.

- Learn to Express Gratitude: If you have a pessimistic mindset, it is easier to forget about all the things in life that are actually going well. The concept of expressing gratitude to those in your life, or even the bed you are sleeping on, the roof over your head, etc., may seem too New Age-like for you. If that is the case, rest assured that research has stated that those who express gratitude on a consisted basis have substantially lower cortisol levels. Being thankful for what you have in life, or simply saying thank you to those around you, also brings the focus off of you, helping you become less self-obsessed and analytical about your own perceived challenges.

- Make the Point to Spend the Time Alone: One of the most important relationships we are going to have is with ourselves. This may sound cliché to some people, but research suggests that if we don't take the time to spend on our own to reflect and inquire about what it is that we want out of life. This is not a selfish task, but a necessary one, if we want to identify the differences between what someone else wants for us, and what others want from us.

- Don't Make Excuses: It is easy to blame other circumstances, as well as other people when things do not entirely go our way in life. But happy and healthy people are able to look at these unfortunate events and take responsibility for them. They are able to look at setbacks as new opportunities, to take a new perspective, to look at issues in a way that always them to thrive, and not to get held back by some perceived 'failures'.

- Focus on Your Strengths: As previously mentioned, no one is going to be good at everything. That doesn't mean though that you cannot be happy with what you know you are good at. Studies have shown that when people participate in activities that play upon their character strengths, they feel happier and less depressed. This doesn't mean though that you should ignore opportunities to try something new, and to completely avoid the activity if you feel you are not 'good enough'. All this habit is looking to instill is the ability to focus on the positive, rather than the negative that constantly make you feel bad about yourself.

- Have Deep Conversations: It is normal to engage in small talk; it is a necessity of life. But studies have shown that the more people spoke about the weather, sports games, and what flavor coffee they like, the more depressed they will feel. It appears that happier people engage in conversations about things that are of more importance, such as politics, mental health issues, and the issues that surround countries and societies outside of our own.

- Engage in Self-Care: Self-care is vital if you want to live a life that is healthy and happy. Happy and healthy people make a point to relax, take care of themselves, and realize that their needs and desires are just as important as the other people in their lives. This may be harder to do for parents, especially mothers, but self-care research over time may have started flipping and popularizing the notion. You cannot always be working or taking care of others; if there is no you, then how can there be we?

- The Experience of Flow: This refers to the ability to be completely absorbed within the present moment. The majority of our problems stem from rumination about the past, and anxiety about the future. Learning to be in the moment may be one of the hardest habits to instill in your life. But if you are able to, it will generally connect you with all of the other habits that have been discussed in this section. Sonja Lyubomirsky writes in her book The How of Happiness:

"The experience of flow leads us to be involved in life (rather than be alienated from it), to enjoy activities (rather than to find them dreary), to have a sense of control (rather than helplessness) and to feel a strong sense of self (rather than unworthiness). All of these factors imbue life with meaning and lend it a richness and intensity. And happiness."

- Celebrate Other's Successes: If we are unhappy in our lives, it is easy to look at others' successes with jealousy and even angry perspective. This expresses itself through insincere expressions of joy or even the act of turning something positive into a negative emotion. Happy and healthy people look at the positive occurrences in another person's life, such as an engagement, a job promotion, the birth of a child, etc., with joy and celebration. They do not take it personally and are genuinely happy for the person and the progress they have made in their lives.

- Practice Mindfulness and Meditation: Mindfulness and meditation are new forms of therapy and self-help skills that have taken the Western World by storm within the past decade. Its benefits are stunning and difficult to ignore. Mindfulness is the art of staying in the moment, and learning to feel your emotions, whether they are positively valance or negatively valance. Meditation is a practice that helps you do this. It has been noted to significantly reduce stress and the existence of various mental health issues.

- Stall the Habit of Overthinking: Rumination is a habit that is responsible for a lot of misery in people's lives. As previously stated, it is connected to the thriving of many mental health issues, as well as general unhappiness. What happy people have learned, through their own suffering, is that ruminating doesn't get them anywhere; it only keeps the loop moving, without and progress forward. Happy people have learned to notice when they are started to ruminate, and choose to act upon a problem or challenge quick, so they no longer have to sit with it in their minds.

- Work on your Health and Happiness: This one sums every good habit up into one; happy and healthy people make their mental and physical health, along with their happiness, a priority. They notice when something isn't working well; if they are unhappy at work, in a relationship, feel negative about everything that happens to them, or simply feel downright blue. They are able to recognize these times and use them as catapults that will send them on the journey of seeking a new and positive way to look at life. They make their happiness a priority and act every day to make sure that they are working in the direction of their most positive and healthy self.

If you recognize any of these habits within yourself, take note of it in your notebook. If you have tried to instill any of these habits before in your life, also, write that down in your notebook. Circle the ones that you would like to try again. Make these the ones that are most related to the bad habits you want to be rid of in your life. The following chapter will teach you how to bring these habits to life, and how to leave the old ways behind.

Chapter 3: Begin Changing Your Habits

It is time now to begin looking at the issues you have with some of your habits in the face and to replace them with more enriching, and greatly positive ones. Do your best to remain judgment-free while you are doing this, and to forgive yourself for any minor setbacks.

Before you begin trying to change certain habits, it may be best to try to assess what level of change you are at.

This is another point where access to your notebook would be helpful.

3.1 The Stages of Change

Look over the list you made of habits you want to instill in your life.

Now, we are going to go through what is called the Stages of Change: The Transtheoretical Model was written in the 1970s by psychologists who were observing people who were trying to quit smoking. They wanted to record the various stages in which they all traveled through that would eventually lead them to take a proactive approach in their healthcare.

The stages are listed as follows:

1. Precontemplation: People in this stage don't plan to take action in the foreseeable future, which is defined as within at least six months. People here are usually not aware that their behavior isn't good for them or others. They are not aware of the many pros that exist should they decide to change their behavior.

2. Contemplation: People in this stage actually begin intended to start down the healthy path in the foreseeable future, at least the next six months. People may not see that their behavior is problematic, and are more thoughtful about the pros that are involved with their decisions to make a change. Some people at this stage though may feel ambivalent toward changing their behavior.

3. Preparation: People are ready in this stage to take action within the next 30 days. People begin taking small steps forward, and believe that this change will help them to live a healthier life.

4. Action: Within this stage, people have taken action to change their behavior and intend to keep moving forward with this change.

5. Maintenance: At this stage, people have been able to sustain their behavior change for at least six months now, and intend to maintain this behavior going forward in their lives. People in this stage also work to prevent relapsing back into old, unhealthy behaviors.

6. Termination: Within this final stage, people have no desire to return back to their unhealthy behavior, and are confident that they are not going to relapse. (This stage is rarely reached as it is very definite; it is usually only used when describing health problems and their changes).

Now look back into your notebook. While referencing the various stages of change, try to write down where you feel you are at with each of them.

You may have already tried something once before, such as trying to exercise at least 3 times a week but relapsed into not exercising at all. You are more than likely going to be at the pre-contemplation or contemplation stage with the majority of the behaviors you want to alter.

Write what you believe about yourself next to the habit you want to change, along with the habit you want to replace it with.

3.2 Actual Neural Rewiring

The use of the word 'rewiring' in this book title wasn't written for show. The science of neurology, which is the study of the brain and how it affects human thought and behavior, has proven that there are various ways that humans can actually reshape the flow of neurons moving through their spine and brain. It was once thought that every person's brain is wired a certain way, and very little can be done about it throughout their lives. Thankfully, through the application of new behaviors and experiences, this is not a fact and something you have vast control over.

Neuroplasticity refers to your brain's ability to reorganize, both physically, functionally, throughout your entire life with influences from the environment, your behavior, thinking, and emotions. Neural pruning refers to the natural process of the brain to extinguish any neuron that isn't being fired. You strengthen certain neural pathways the more you engage in the same thought patterns, behavior, emotions, interactions, etc. This is essentially how learning a new skill works; you start off one way, and if you participate in this hobby on a consistent basis, the neural pathway that is associated with it will become stronger, warmer, and more instantly activated.

This process is the key to understanding how instilling new habits work. There is a reason why when you tried to stretch your injured muscles only three times last week, then forgot one week, and then only did it twice another, that this behavior did not become a habit. The neural pathway simply wasn't warm enough, and neurons are only going to fire when they are being summoned often.

A quote from Dr. Michael Merzenich from his book *Soft-Wired: How the New Science of Brain Plasticity Can Change Your Life*, highlights the complete control every person has sitting between their skull:

"Whatever the circumstances of a child's early life, and whatever the history and current state of that child, every human has the built-in power to improve, to

change for the better, to significantly restore and often to recover. Tomorrow, that person you see in the mirror can be a stronger, more capable, livelier, more powerfully centered, and still-growing person."

So if you get stuck and feel irritated about why your new habit isn't sticking, thinking about the various neural pathways running through your brain. Also, try to think about how warm those pathways are that are going in the direction of the old behaviors.

A study was conducted in London that aimed to find out exactly how long it takes for someone to instill a new, automatic habit into their lives. This study was led by Phillippa Lally, a health psychology researcher at University College London. They examined the habits of 96 people over a 12-week period. Each person chose one new habit for the 12 weeks they were being observed, and each reported every day on whether or not they did the behavior, and how automatic that behavior felt. On average, it takes a person more than 2 months to act upon the same behavior before it biomes automatic. 66 days, was the specific number.

Give yourself at least two months, or even more, before you begin feeling hopeless. Even then, it took some other people in the study a lot more time to make their habit automatic—but this greatly depended upon a person's personality, circumstances, and history of trying to instill the same habit.

3.3 Steps to Take to Begin Creating New Habits

The following is a template that you can apply to any of the habits that you want to create for yourself, along with the ones you want to get rid of. Read this section over a few times before writing it out again in your notebook, for each new habit that you want to form.

1. Identify Cues: There is something that has to trigger a habit, and a cue can be really anything that relates to it; maybe stress makes you want food, alcohol, or a certain thought or post on social media makes you want to procrastinate. Whatever it may be, try to notice these. If this is hard for you to do, try to notice when you are engaging in a bad habit, and then going back from there. Did someone say something to you? Did you read something on the internet? Are you

worried about something? Do you best to honestly reflect yourself.

2. Disrupt: Once you have noticed the cues that are triggering your chosen bad habit, you can begin trying to throw it off. For example, if reading something on social media makes you feel bad about yourself and your skills, which makes you want to sit on the couch and procrastinate, try limiting your social media activity, or at least not doing it in the morning or the time you feel most affected.

3. Replace: Research has shown that if you have a more positive habit in mind to replace a bad one, you are more likely to stop participating in the bad one. The new habit interferes with the old one, making it harder for your brain to go on autopilot and go down the path with those warm neural pathways. A good example of this is trying to replace night-time snacks with fruit or something healthier; not having junk food available may also be another step in disarming that bad eating habit.

4. Keep it Simple: Making new behaviors simply goes in line with the old behaviors; those were

easy too, which is why you have engaged in them for so long. Making a new habit too difficult will make the application of it far less appealing.

5. Think Long Term: Habits generally form because they satisfy short-term impulses. The results though of these short-term impulses may last a while though, such as avoiding cleaning the dishes or stretching your injured leg. When you are engaging in new habits, try to think about the long term effects that this will have on your life, and how you are doing it for the best for yourself.

6. Persist: Habits are hard to break; that's why there are so many books written about forming new ones! We order in at night because it is easy, and we don't want to make dinner. This may be because we had a long, tiring day at work, and/or we did not bring enough food for lunch and can't be bothered to rummage up a home-cooked meal. We also may have no brought the right amount of food for lunch because we did not plan ahead the night before, staying up late and lying on the couch. This kind of habit connects to many other bad habits, so, if we look at this as an example, where to begin would be to start making lunches

for the week that are substantial enough to feel full of. Then, at the end of the day, you will have more energy to actually cook a healthier, financially sound dinner.

Instilling a new habit is going to take time. While you are looking over your list of new behavioral habits to apply, take a glance at this next list, which will give you advice on how you can improve your mental strength while putting in the effort to make healthier, happier choices

1. Create Behavioral Experiments to Challenge Your Self-Limiting Beliefs: There is probably more than one reason why you haven't been able to keep up with a certain habit in your life. You may suffer from mental health disorders, or even have become used to self-diminishing dialogue. Whatever it may be, it doesn't make you less capable than anyone else or mean that you possess less mental strength than other people. Your self-limiting beliefs are simply trying to convince you of these lies. As previously stated, some of these self-limiting beliefs have the ability to turn into self-fulfilling prophecies, because you

are only expecting a negative result, or that no one is going to like you. So you may need to change those first before you start looking at behavioral habits. There will be a section in a later chapter that offers various exercises that can help you with this very task.

2. Replace Victim Language with Empowering Statements: Self-limiting beliefs are more than likely going to be made worse by the constant use of victim language. You may employ this within your self-dialogue on the daily. If you catch yourself blaming others for how you feel, or the negative circumstances in your life, stop yourself. This is the victim language. It makes you feel like you are not in control of your daily life. Try to replace it with statements that you feel like you ARE in control; because you are! You deserve to recognize that you are in the driver's seat of the life that you are living in.

3. Practice Self-Compassion: Calling yourself names and putting yourself down isn't going to motivate you to try again, or to try anything else that is challenging for the matter. If you want to do better, think about how you would talk to

someone you love after they make a mistake or something negative happens in their lives. If you are a reasonable person, you wouldn't sit and insult them for hours on end. You would show them compassion, empathy, and support them into making new decisions about the future. Try to do this for yourself, and recognize that this is only going to help you in the long run, as bringing yourself down is only going to make you feel unhealthier and unhappy.

4. Behave like the Person You Want to Become: Wishing that you could be a certain way isn't going to make it happen. Wishing that you could be a morning person or a person that exercises daily, isn't going to do anything, but make you feel bad for yourself. You are capable of becoming these things, and the first step toward that becoming is trying to act like that person. Ask yourself, what would a morning person too? And follow through on those answers.

5. Live in The Moment: This is going to be a repeated notion throughout this book, as lack of living the moment is a consistent cause of unhappiness, lack of health, and various mental

health disorders. Staying within the moment and getting what you can out of it is the only way that you can improve yourself, and reach the future that you have been planning for. Mindfulness and meditation will be discussed as well, later in this book.

Since there are many habits that people, in general, want to instill in these lives, this book will explore some of the more common and pervasive habits that can help you're as a whole. What will be covered in the rest of this chapter will be the habit of creating boundaries, becoming more assertive, learning how to constructively problem solve, and how to how to stick to certain daily schedules.

Chapter 4: Creating Boundaries

One of the main habits that people with low self-esteem tend to fall into the habit of saying 'yes' too often. These are people pleasers, who either say 'yes' to tasks at work, or 'yes' to family and friends, to things that they within their mind really don't want to do. Before you try to become more assertive, you may have to practice creating and maintaining boundaries with certain people in your life. A lot of people may not know what creating boundaries means, or how to begin doing so. Should you be one of those people, this section will help you take a glance inside and comprehend just what building boundaries might mean to you.

1. Name Your Limits: First, you need to tune into your mental, emotionally, and possibly spiritual limits. You can't try to build boundaries without recognizing this. Observe yourself, and consider what you can tolerate, and learn to accept the things that make you feel stressed and uncomfortable. Those feelings will help you understand where you limit lie.

2. Tune into your Feelings: There are several feelings that arise that may be important for

helping you to notice when your boundaries are being crossed. The main ones are the sensations of discomfort and resentment. Try to think of these feelings on a continuum from 1 to 10. 10 would act as the higher level of sensation. If you are feeling one of these emotions on the high scale, try to ask yourself what is causing them; what is it about the moment, the interaction, that is making you feel this way? Is it the person, or their expectation? When you first start observing yourself, try to make note of it in your notebook, so you can recall it, should you feel this feeling again. Resentment comes from feeling like you are being taken advantage of, and a sign that you are being pushed beyond the limits you possess. It is also because we feel guilty if we do not grant this request from a person that we care about. We worry that it will affect our relationship with them and that we will no longer be valued.

3. Be Direct: If you do not have boundaries, and have difficulties being assertive with people, then being direct is going to be hard for you. Depending upon the relationship you have with the person, you have not had to be so direct in

dialogue while you are trying to establish these boundaries. But there may be others who are not like you in your life, and of whom you need to be more straight-forward with. An example of this difference may sound something like this: you have no problem having a friendly disagreement with a sibling about politics, while your sister-in-law feels uncomfortable having this discussion. This could be crossing her own personal boundaries. Time, as another example, is a topic within a romantic relationship that may be involved within the conversation of boundaries. Some couples need to have a direct talk about how much time is needed on their own in order to maintain a thorough sense of sense, as well as how much time is needed together to feel intimate.

4. Give Yourself Permission: When you first begin to instill this habit, it is more than likely that you may feel feelings of guilt, even if you are feeling taken advantage of. You may feel like you are a bad partner, a bad daughter or son while setting boundaries with family members. But try to remember this; setting boundaries is healthy, and

a sign of self-respect. If you have never tried to create boundaries for yourself, then those around you may not be used to it, so try to give them time to settle in. If it's easier, you can practice being direct and telling them that you are trying to make boundaries for your own mental health.

5. Practice Self-Awareness: Self-awareness is going to be key in instilling new habits in general. You have to try to become more aware of how you are feeling, as well as the physical reactions in your body. Try to listen to these occurrences, and not judge or criticize them for existing. If you notice yourself slipping and not maintaining your boundaries, try to maintain observation, and ask yourself some more questions, such as "What is the situation that is making me feel resentful and stressed?" You can then go over your options, what you can proactively do about the situation. Try to focus only on what you have control over.

6. Consider your Past and Present: If you haven't ever created boundaries, it may be time to look into your past and reflect on how others in your life have affected this influence. If you grew up as the caretaker, you may have grown up thinking

that it is your responsibility to take care of others, and thus drain yourself of energy and emotions. Notice this, and accept it. Note now, that you are not going to do that anymore. Try to think about the people you surround yourself with, and how they influence your opinion on setting boundaries. Think about whether or not your important relationships are balanced, give and take. Take a look at your environment as well, such as your work; many work environments expect you to 'go above and beyond', which is often unhealthy. If you are trying to maintain boundaries in your work life, it may appear to others that you are not working 'as hard'. But the truth is, you are trying to take care of yourself. Reflect on how this makes you feel at work.

7. Make Self-Care a Priority: This concept will be discussed extensively in another chapter. But self-care is important when trying to instilling boundaries, especially when you are tuning in to your emotions. Putting yourself first requires a lot of mental energy, especially when you are starting off with them in several sections of your life.

8. Seeking Support: If you are having a hard time setting boundaries, try to seek out support from others, like a good friend or family member. It may be better to seek support from people who are outside the people of whom you are building boundaries with, so they can act as a third party. There are also many self-help books you can use should you want to follow along on your own.

9. Be Assertive: This strategy will be discussed more extensively in the next section, but it very important to maintain boundaries by being assertive. There are some people who are not used to you acting this way, in favor of your own desires and needs, so you are likely to receive a lot of push back early on. Stick to your guns though, and do your best not to allow them to make you feel guilty. Try to remember this; you are not being selfish or aggressive by letting people know that you are only going to participate in what makes you feel comfortable.

10. Start Small: Assertively communicating your boundaries is going to feel difficult at first. If trying to create boundaries with your parents, who show up without notice at your apartment on

the weekends, feels too large, experts have suggested that it may be best to start smaller. So within your little notebook, write a hierarchy of boundaries, starting with the smallest, least threatening boundary you want to instill into your life. Then slowly work your way up from there, constantly looking through this list should you feel a setback or lack of confidence in the new habit you are instilling.

Chapter 5: Becoming More Assertive

As previously mentioned, there is a big difference between being aggressive and controlling, then choosing to be confident when validating your needs and desires. Therefore, there is a difference between expressing anger aggressively and assertively. Expressing your anger assertively means that you are able to express how you feel while being in control of the feelings you are experiencing. Learning to express yourself assertively means separately how you feel with how you express yourself.

If you are having difficulty identifying the differences between being assertive and being aggressive, try to read over these basic summaries:

- Assertiveness is based on balance: It requires being straightforward about your wants and needs, while still considering these wants and needs of others. You are still applying empathy while firmly getting how you feel across to another person.

- Aggressive behavior is based on winning: You focus solely on what is in your best interest without thinking about the needs and desires of others. The power you are applying while being aggressive is strictly selfish. You will come across as being a bully or pushy.

MindTools.com identifies seven suggested steps that you can follow if you want to develop your assertiveness skills. Applying these will help you to feel more balanced:

Value Yourself and Your Rights: Before you try to become more assertive, you should gain a better understanding of yourself. You should also try to develop a strong belief in your natural value of self, as well as your value within a team. Confidence is important when trying to be more assertive, but try not to allow it to turn into a sense of self-importance. Your needs, desires, and rights are just as important as everyone else's.

Voice Your Needs and Wants Confidently: If you want to perform at your best level and feel happy in life, you need to make sure your needs and wants are met. Try to identify the things that you want and need now. Set goals (as mentioned in the previous section) so you can look forward to achieving them. Once you have done this, it will be easier to express what you need or want.

Remember to ask politely, stick to your point, and not to ask others to sacrifice their own needs for yours.

Acknowledge That You Can't Control Other People's Behaviors: This is an important fact for those with anger issues to realize. Oftentimes, we become angry with people when they do things that do not line up with what we want. But we cannot control what other people do, and it is important to keep reminding yourself of that fact. You can only focus on your own behavior. As long as you are respecting the needs of others, then you have the right to say what you want.

Learn to Express Yourself in a Positive Way: Falling into negative behaviors and expressions of anger is very easy. Try to focus on expressing what you need positively, even if you are feeling angry. This will help you not fall into the bad habit of name-calling, accusing, etc.

Be Open to Criticism and Compliments: Try to develop the skill of accepting both positive and negative feedback. Sometimes, when you receive negative feedback, it is easy to start feeling defensive and even hurt. If you do not agree with the feedback you are receiving, then you need to prepare yourself to say so.

Again, this is meant to be expressed assertively, without anger or aggressiveness.

Learn to Say No: People who suffer from issues when being assertive often have difficulty saying no. Saying no is important when considering your own wants and needs, as well as contracting boundaries that are healthy and necessary. You are not able to please everyone, nor are you and endless source of energy. Saying no to people in your relationships, job settings, and friends show that you know what you want and need, and respect yourself enough to follow through on them.

Using Assertive Communication Techniques: There are a number of ways that you can apply certain assertive skills through the practice of some of these strategies:

- Use "I" Statements: Using the word "I" conveys the basic assertion that you want to get your point across firmly. It also avoids blaming and the escalation of pointless arguments.

- Empathy: It is hard when you are angry to try to see the issues from another person's point of view. But if you practice empathy on a consistent basis, the level in which your anger reaches will begin to lower each time you feel you are going to overreact. If you see a situation from another person's point of view, it is easier to understand the reasoning behind their behavior. You still don't have to agree with the person, but it will help your anger feel more constructive rather than destructive.

- Escalation: Trying to be assertive with another person isn't always going to work the first time you apply it. Maybe that person also has issues with anger and expressing themselves/Some problems also require more time and patience in order to be resolved, such as problems in the workplace. If you feel you need to escalate your assertiveness, continue along the path of being polite and respectful, but firm.

- Ask for more Time: If you can feel your anger rising and identify that you are having trouble controlling it, feel enough confidence to ask for some time so your anger can dissipate, and you can choose a reaction that is more rational.

- Change Your Verbs: Try integrated verbs into your vocabulary that clearly and firmly state what it is your asking for, or what it is that you need. When you do this, there will be more room for misinterpretation. Begin using words like "will" instead of "could/should", and "want" instead of "need", "choose to" instead of "have to".

- Don't be afraid to sound like a Broken Record: Keep reiterating yourself if a person is not taking what you are saying seriously. Continue you using the strong and firm message until the person will realize that you are drawing a line and are meaning what you're saying. This is best to practice at work if you are overwhelmed with tasks, and someone tries to throw more onto, using guilt as a weapon. No matter what they say, stick with your assertive statement that lets them know you cannot take on any more work. Your needs are important.

- Try Scripting: Scripting is a technique that allows you to practice making assertive statements before you may need to state them. It will help you prepare what you are going to say, and give you enough confidence to stick to it:

The Event: Tell the other person exactly how you see the issue.

Your Feelings: Describe how you feel about the situation and express them as clearly as possible.

Your needs: Tell the person exactly what it is that you need from them so they do not have to guess.

The Consequences: Describe the positive effect that your request will have for the other person if you need are actually met.

Write down the observe steps in your notebook if this is an occurrence you want to practice being assertive about. Applying assertiveness instead of being angry will, in the long run, help you in your relationships, your work life, and will help you live a more enjoyable and fulfilling life.

Chapter 6: How to Constructively and Effectively Problem Solve

6.1 Identifying Your Problems

Make a list of the problems you are currently facing. List as many or as little as you would like. Begin by not going into too much detail. Some suggested words that may help you summarize the problem are: relationship with family or spouse, loss or death or someone close, isolation/loneliness, unemployment, harassment or abuse, financial issues, legal issues, substance use issues, physical or mental health issues, low self-esteem or confidence.

1._____

2._____

3._____

4._____

5._____

Next, still, on this same step, choose a problem that you would like to work on from your list.

Once you have chosen one, ask yourself these questions to help you define the problem more clearly:

Why is this a problem? What effect does it have on my life?

What is the problem?

When does this problem occur?

Where does the problem occur?

Who is involved in this problem?

Once you have answered these questions, try to write out a single sentence that summarizes the problem. Start your statement with the word "I", and include an action word within it.

If you do not have control over the problem, then it is going to be difficult to resolve it. Try to choose problems from your list that you have some level of control over.

6.2 Generating Solutions

Use this section to write down potential solutions for the problem you have just selected. Don't worry for now about whether or not this problem seems realistic or practical. Try not to think too much about it. No matter what ideas come to mind, write them down.

After you have finished writing down all of your potential solutions, take some time to evaluate your list. Eliminate those that are too hard or involve solutions that are not realistic, or involves elements that you are not in control of. Look out for duplicates of solutions.

Choose the best looking ideas that you feel are most practical and likely for you to commit to.

Now it is time for you to evaluate your idea, by weighing out the advantages, disadvantages and neutral components of implementing this solution. Need be, to help you write these out, ask yourself the following questions:

How will this solution affect my own well-being? (This means how it will affect you physically, emotionally, and psychologically).

How much effort and time is needed?

Are there any financial risks involved?

Does it fit in with my other daily routines and goals?

How will it affect those around me?

Is this a feasible solution?

Advantages: _____

Disadvantages: _____

Neutral thoughts: _____

If your idea for a solution has more advantages or neutral thoughts than disadvantages, write out a final statement of this solution. If it does not, go back to your list and solutions and try to find one that has more potential to it.

6.3 Making an Action Plan

This section will clearly define the steps that you need to take in order to make your proposed solution work in the real world. The more clear that you write out an action plan, the more likely that it is going to succeed. This will make it easier to attack the problem head-on and to have something to refer back to when you begin to have trouble.

My Problem is: _____

My Solution is: _____

My plan to do this is: _____

Write out as many steps as you feel may be necessary in order to complete solving your problem.

6.4 Review your Progress

Reviewing your progress is an important part of becoming an expert in applying Structured Problem Solving. With every step laid out clearly and concise, you develop a more natural skill of assessing and revolving problems. You will learn as much from your mistakes as you will from your successes. Ask yourself, when reviewing your progress:

What worked well?

What didn't work as planned?

What would I change about my plan?

Once you have made your way through this entire section, give yourself a pat on the back! You have taken a big step toward proactively solving issues in your life.

If you feel like you have successfully solved the problem, try to go through the list and apply these steps toward each problem. Even if you have to go through this problem-solving section a few times with one problem, try not to be too hard on yourself. There is a reason that they are called problems in the first place

Chapter 7: Scheduling and Setting Personal Goals

7.1 Instilling Scheduling

One of the main barriers to instilling new habits and helping us feel productive is not having a proper schedule in place. This doesn't mean that it has to be a rigid schedule that you follow to at, but even having a vague idea in mind can not only save you a lot of time but help you feel like you got a lot done, which in turn, inspires us to do more. There are only 24 hours in a day, and of course, this section still applies to those who tend to overwork; those individuals have also not put a proper schedule in place, because they are rushing and shoving too much to do within a small time period.

Scheduling, in essence, is the art of planning a reasonable amount of activities within a reasonable time period. This means that you do not overwork, nor do you underwork. When it is done effectively, the following results are achieved:

- You can understand what you realistically achieve with your time.

- Make sure you have enough time for essential tasks.

- Add adjustments for things that are unexpected.

- Helps you avoid more than you can handle.

- It helps you work steadily toward both personal and career-oriented goals.

- You'll have enough time for both your family friends, exercise, hobbies, and work-life.

- You will achieve a healthy work-life balance.

The following are steps that you can take to start effectively scheduling your time. These are written in accordance with advice taken from *MindTools.com*.

First of all, you have to set a regular time/day to actually make your schedule. It can be on the first of your week or month. There is an abundant amount of tools that you can utilize in order to get this first task done. A simple way of doing this is to use a pen and paper, and buying a weekly planner notebook (or even downloading ones from the internet. It is recommended more though that you put it in one place, such as a notebook, to avoid losing the sheets of paper and to stay more organized.) There are also various apps such as Google Calendar, MS Outlook, and other apps on your specific evidence you can look for. The most important aspect of choosing your planner is that it allows you to view the appropriate amount of time, and the level of detail that you require. Once you have that, then you can begin following these steps:

Step 1: Identify Available Time: Begin by establishing the time you want to make available for your work life. How much time you spend at work should reflect the kind of job you have, as well as the personal goals outside of work that you want to achieve. It depends what you prefer, and what phase of your life you are in. Identify your priorities. For example, if you want to spend more time with family, then it may be better to place your time into that and organize the time off work more reasonably. If you are working toward a promotion, you may need to put in more time for work than you usually do, so you allot more time for yourself within that week or month for yourself.

Step 2: Block in the actions you absolutely must do in order to do a good job. These are usually the things that you are assessed within your job type. This, of course, will depend on what kind of job you have, so take that into consideration.

Step 3: Try to make a to-do list, and schedule in high-priority and urgent activates, as well as maintenance tasks that are important, that cannot be delegated or avoided. Try to arrange these for the times of day when you are the most productive. Some people are the most energized in the morning, while others do better in the afternoon. If you are unsure about which time of day you are most efficient, try to observe your mood and motivation during the day.

There are likely going to be interruptions during your day that you cannot predict. Try to leave some open space in your schedule for these issues that are inevitable to arise.

Step 5: Schedule Discretionary Time: The space that is left in your planner will be called 'discretionary time'; this is the time that is available to deliver your priorities and achieve your goals. Review your personal goals and to-do list, and add them into this leftover time if you are able to do it. Do not squish it in though.

Step 6: Analyze Your Activities: If you have gone through your to-do list, or are feeling rush, or are not able to get everything done that is needed, you need to go through these steps again. One of the most important things you can do to build success is my maximizing the leverage you can achieve with your time. You can increase your level of productivity by delegating at work or using technology to automate much of your work as possible.

Here are other ways that you can begin prioritizing your workload and personal goals. Here is how to create and follow through on a to-do list:

1. Write down all of the tasks you need to complete. If they are large tasks, break out the first action step, and write this down with the larger tasks. You may find it easier to create multiple lists and steps for each task you want to achieve.

2. Run through these tasks and allocate them by priorities from A, which is very important or urge, to F, which are unimportant and not very urgent.

Simply work through your list in order, prioritizing a first, and then so on.

7.2 Setting Personal Goals

The following will discuss life goals in general, which may include less to do with career-oriented ones. You can create your big-picture goals, which are vaguer and over a lifetime (or at least the next 10 years). Then eventually you can break these down into smaller and smaller targets that you will hit until you reach those life goals. You can achieve all of this by creating a specific plan, that is reasonable and most simple.

1. First, you need to think about what you want to achieve in your lifetime, or by a significant amount of time. If you set lifetime goals to give you the overall perspective to think about as you move forward, as you meet small goals and keep moving onto what you want.

   Here are a few categories you can create so you write down the goals you want to achieve in each category of your life:

- Career: What level do you want to reach in your career? What do you want to achieve? How much of your time do you want to spend at your job?

- Financial: How much do you want to earn in life, and at what point? Is this related to your career goals or is it not?

- Educational: Is there a set of skills you would like to learn? Or a particular level of education you would like to achieve?

- Family: Do you want to be a parent? If so, what kind of parent are you going to be? How are you going to do this?

- Artistic: Do you want to achieve any artistic goals? How are you going to do this?

- Attitude: Do you have a certain mindset holding you back? Do you lack confidence? How do you want to help yourself get away from these attitudes?

- Physical: Are there any athletic goals that you want to achieve, or do you want good health for the rest of your life? What steps are going to take to achieve this?

- Pleasure: How do you want to enjoy yourself? How are you going to make time for yourself for that?

- Public Service: Are you going to try to make the world a better place? Are you going to set goals for this as well?

2. Setting Smaller Goals: Once you have set some serious lifetime goals, you can start making a five-year plan for some smaller ones. These are the goals you set that will help you achieve your lifetime ones. Next, you make a one-year plan, a six-month plan, and a one-month plan that gets progressively smaller and smaller. Each should be based on the previous plan. Then you can create a to-do list of these things that can help you on a daily basis to reach these goals.

The first few things you do may involve gathering information about achieving your higher goals. This will help you to improve the quality and how realistic the goals you have set truly are.

A useful way of making goals more powerful is to use the SMART goals method. It stands for:

S - Specific (or significant)

M - Measurable (or meaningful)

A - Attainable (or action-oriented)

R - Relevant (or rewarding)

T - Time-bound (or tractable.

If you have a goal that is too general, the SMART way of setting goals will help you make it more specific. For example, if one of your goals is to travel around Europe, a SMART goal would state when you want to have it done by, what year you want to do it, and the following, smaller goals that are required in order for you to achieve this (such as saving money, booking the trip, going solo or with others, etc.)

7.3 More Tips for Setting Goals

- State each goal as a Positive Statement: Express your goals in a positive manner, that helps the goal feel more achievable and desirable. It also helps you maintain a positive outlook on life and a better way of thinking about yourself.

- Be Precise: It is easier to achieve goals if you are more specific about them. Place certain dates and times that you want to do them, and have them achieved by. If you do this you will have them in mind and will work harder in order to achieve those goals by those times. You will be satisfied with the one you are able to do this.

- Set Priorities: You can also prioritize each goal so you do not feel overwhelmed by them. This will help you direct your attention toward the ones that are more important than others.

- Write Goals Down: This gives them more power and allows you to remember them more.

- Keep Operational Goals Small: Keep the low-level goals that you're working towards small and very achievable. If a goal is too large, then it may make you feel less motivated toward achieving it.

- Set Performance Goals, not Outcome Goals: You should try to set goals that you have control over, as opposed to the ones that you do not. Try to base them on your own personal growth, which are things that are under your control. For example, getting a promotion is more under your control, where buying a house may not be, due to the housing market and the amount of money you have at that time.

Chapter 8: Gaining Control of Your Emotions

Sometimes we are not able to achieve our goals or are able to create new habits because we have certain emotional issues that get in our way. Whether it be due to certain mental health issues, or simply a sensitivity, reacting to your emotions is a habit in itself, one that is learned, and can easily be unlearned.

Feeling emotional is not a bad thing. It is only when our emotions are left unchecked and unexpressed that they begin to interfere with our daily activities and goals. There are many ways that you can learn how to more regulate your emotions in a healthier manner, but before we get to that, we will discuss the importance of self-care and various relaxation techniques

8.1 The Importance of Self-Care

Various studies within the past few years have learned the importance of self-care and how it affects our productivity and performances in life. What self-care is essential, is the time that we take to relax and participate in activities and hobbies that we enjoy.

It can be things like getting a massage, getting your nails done, or it can anything as simple as scheduling time to watch a good movie. Here is a list of the various benefits of self-care on your mental and physical health, as well as various reasons as to why integrating self-care into your life is important:

- Knowing Your Worth: Self-care reminds you that maintaining a healthy relationship with yourself produces positive feels and boosts your confidence and self-esteem. It also tells you that your needs and desires are as important as others.

- A Healthy Work-Life Balance: Contrary to what many people believe, over-working is not a virtue. Accompanying this activity is an unhealthy amount of stress, less productivity, and disorganized emotional development. Overworking can lead to all kinds of mental and physical health problems, such as anxiety and depression, insomnia, and heart disease. Self-care can range from activities outside of work to ones at work, such as making sure you take your breaks, avoiding overextending, and setting professional boundaries.

- Stress Management: Constant stress and anxiety, as previously stated, is incredibly unhealthy. There is such a thing as a normal amount of stress because it can inspire you to achieve your goals and move forward. Self-care helps you recharge your batteries and allows you to face your goals in a more relaxed and productive manner.

- Start Living, Stop Existing: Everyone has a lot of responsibilities, which means they are things that we have to do in life. They are not always things that we enjoy, such as paying bills, fixing the dryer, and doing the dishes, but once we take the time for self-care, we realize that self-care is also a responsibility. Taking the time for things you enjoy helps you get up in the morning, and have things to look forward to when there are a lot of things in life that we have to do.

- Better Physical Health: Your physical health will benefit while your mental health does because you have made the choice to participate in physical exercise, eat better, get a good amount of sleep, and take care of your hygiene.

Here are 10 simple self-care habits you can easily start blending into your life:

1. Go for a run, a light jog, or a scenic walk in the woods.

2. Take a break when you need it. Whether it at work or during social interaction.

3. Choose who you spend time with.

4. Eat green foods daily; it is great for both your mental and physical health.

5. Avoid emotional eating.

6. Start a journal (this is different than your notebook; it'll be more diary-style than the notebook where you write down your new habits.)

7. Learn to say 'no'.

8. Stop overthinking.

9. Laugh heartily at least once a day.

10. Meditate or do deep breathing once a day.

Speaking of meditation, the following section is going to go over various deep breathing and relaxation strategies that you can blend into your day to help you feel calmer. You don't have to be a monk and sit for hours on end in order to receive the various benefits that come with deep relaxation and meditation. Take about 20 minutes out of your day, and try to note how you are feeling both before, and after. Certain techniques may appeal to you more than others, so feel free to go over a few of them more than once in order to find what suits you.

8.2 Relaxed Breath Techniques

The point of breathing exercises and relaxation strategies is not to replace the sensation of anxiety, depression or anger, or to run from it, but to embrace it, and help you learn the difference between thoughts and physical sensations. These strategies will help you become more aware of how your body reacts to certain thoughts and moods. Please take note of when you feel you may be using one of those strategies in order to flee from the unpleasant feeling. This is not the point of them, and will only injure your progress in the long run.

8.3 Breathing Exercises: Slow Diaphragmatic Breathing

This technique sends a direct signal to the brain to let it know that it is safe. This practice is usually recommended to be done alone, either before you start your day or after it. You can apply it while you are in a situation that makes you anxious, or are coping with memory or triggered depressive thoughts. But remember, you are not doing this to rid yourself of the anxiety. If you are doing it at the moment, remember that it is meant to have the emotion felt, and to remind you that you are safe.

From a comfortable chair with your feet on the floor, or find a place to lie down.

Place your hands onto your belly and allow them to rest gently.

Start by observing your breath. Try not to judge the pace in which your belly is rising and falling.

Begin filling up your belly with an inhale slow, so it starts to feel like a little beach ball or globe. Imagine a balloon being filled up. Do not do this roughly or too fast. Focus on breathing into your stomach, and not allowing your shoulders to lift as you inhale.

Breathe out slowly to the count of five. Try to do this as slowly as possible.

After the exhale, hold for about 2-3 seconds before you inhale into your belly again.

Breathe in and out this way and observe how your breath has slowed down.
Practice this for around 10 minutes.

This practice will work better if you try to do this twice a day at the beginning of your treatment. Try to do it at the same point of the day, every day. This is usually a good start for those who suffer from anxiety or anger issues.

8.4 Progressive Muscle Relaxation

Many people with anxiety, depression and anger issues suffer from muscle tension. For the person with anxiety, it is because when they experience the emotion of that anxiety in their body, their muscle tense up, as a reaction toward a perceived threat (to either participate in fight or flight). People with repressed anger issues suffer from the same problem. Those with depression are known to possess extra tense muscles because of the constant ruminating that causes immense stress within their bodies.

For whatever reason it may be, this technique attempts to employ the opposite. It is the absence of tension in the body's muscles. The aim of it is to gradually learn to release tension in the muscles through daily exercise. This shows your body during moments of anxiety and/or anger that you are safe, and reduces the likelihood of a flight or fight response.

The practice has you systematically tensing and relaxing certain muscle groups of the body. If you try it out for a moment and tense your bicep now, for about 5-7 seconds, then allow it to relax, you feel the instant difference in the lack of tension.

If you have a history of other medical problems, please consult with your local physician about using this relaxation exercise:

You will be stating at your feet and working your way up to your face. Make yourself comfortable with loose clothing, and either sit upright on a chair or lie down.

Take a few minutes to breathe in and out slowly, with deep breaths.

When you feel ready, shift your attention to your right foot. Observe it without judgment.

Slowly, begin tensing the muscles in your right foot, squeezing as tightly as you are physically able to. Hold for a count to 10.

Slowly relax your foot. Focus on the tension slowly leaking out as your foot gets loose and limp.

Stay in this moment for a few seconds, breathing slowly and deeply.

Shift your attention to your left foot.

Follow these steps for each section of your body.

If you are unsure about which muscles you should tense at the same or separate moment, try following this miniature guideline:

- Right foot, left foot.

- Right calf, left calf.

- Right thigh, left thigh.

- Buttocks and hips.

- Stomach.

- Chest.

- Back.

- Right arm and hand, left arm and hand.

- Shoulders and neck.

- Face.

It may take some time for you to adjust to tensing the right body muscles, but do not be too hard on yourself. You are slowly teaching your body to calm down.

8.5 Body Scan Meditation

This meditation is a relaxed breath technique that blends together concepts of progressive muscle relaxation and deep breathing. It focuses your attention on various parts of your body as well, but instead of tensing and relaxing them, you will simply focus on the way each part of your body feels, and avoid labeling the sensations as something positive or negative.

Lie on your back with your legs uncrossed, arms relaxed at your sides. You can have your eyes either open or closed, but if they are open, try not to focus on anything in particular. Focus on your breathing for about two minutes so you can become relaxed.

Begin by focusing on the toes of your right foot. Notice any sensations that might be lurking there, whether it be tingling, an itch, or nothing at all. Focus on it while imagining each deep breath flowing through your toes. Stay on this area for about 1-2 minutes.

Move onto the sole of your foot. Then move onto the right foot and repeat.

Move to your calf, knee, thigh, hip on your right side. Then the left side.

Once you have observed both sides, practice this observation on your torso, lower back and abdomen, the upper back and chest, and shoulders. Finally, end on your neck, your face, and the top of your head.

Once you have focused on each part of your body for around 1-2 minutes each, relax for a while in silence and stillness, noticing how your body is feeling.

Slowly open your eyes.

This form of meditation teaches you that whatever you may be feeling your body is fine as it is, and does not require a label that falls under the category of either bad or good. This is an attempt to retrain your mind and no longer find negative associations between certain bodily sensations and the anticipation of oncoming doom.

8.6 Mindfulness: The Benefits

Mindfulness is a practice that has grown in popularity and is often integrated into various forms of therapeutic treatment. Mindfulness is defined as a practice that longs to keep you in the present moment without the desire to flee from whatever feeling, bodily sensation, or behavioral issue may be plaguing you. Many mental health issues thrive on either dwelling on the past or obsessing over the future. Mindfulness practices help you learn to observe your thoughts without judgment or criticism and to teach you how to begin cultivating compassion toward yourself and your experiences.

8.7 Mindfulness Meditation

Mindfulness meditation is not just meant for monks. Many people misunderstand what the point of mindful meditation is. An image of someone hovering over the clouds on a mountaintop is a commonly associated misconception. Mindfulness meditation is not practice meant for an elect few. It is meant to be practice by anyone and everyone, no matter what age or point they are in their lives. No matter how busy, stressed, anxious, angry, or unhappy you may be, mindfulness meditation will act as another tool to integrate into your self-care toolbox. It has been successful to help people in the past reduce stress, anxiety, depression, and anger issues.

Depending on what kind of mindfulness meditation you are participating in, the practice will help you by focusing your attention either on a single repetitive action, such as breathing or encourage you to observe a specific portion of your mind. Some practices ask you to observe your thoughts without judgment or criticism, so you can learn that thoughts are just as they are; not you at all. It can also be applied to several activities that involve movement, such as walking, eating, or exercising.

Here is a simple exercise of mindful meditation that you can begin practicing now:

Find a quiet, comfortable space where you know you will not be interrupted or distracted.

Sit on a chair that is straight-backed, or sit crossed-legged on the floor.

Choose a point of focus; most people like to focus on their breathing at first. It can be the sensation of air moving in and out of your nostrils, your belly rising and falling, or a candle flame or meaningful word you repeated through the practice.

Distracting thoughts do not mean you are 'doing it wrong'. Your mind is like a monkey and is meant to be playing around. If you find yourself becoming distracted, do not be angry. The point is to simply bring your attention back to the selected focus of attention, no matter how many times your mind tries to run off.

8.8 Visualization

This is a guided imagery practice and a variation on tradition mediation that involves the imagining of a scene that helps you to feel calm. Each person will have a different scene that makes them feel calm; it can be a beach, a childhood home, or even just your bed at home. You can do visualization either on your own or with a therapist. Aids such as soothing music help some people visualize better, along with sounds that co-inside with your particular location.

Here is an easy visualization exercise that can help you get started:

Close your eyes. Be sure to do this in a place where you are not distracted or unsafe.

Find music, sounds, or rhythmic tones that will help your experience feel more authentic. These can be found through YouTube, or through a simple google search.

Picture your peaceful place as vividly as you can; make note of the sounds, sights, smells, feels, and tastes.

Some people lose track of where they are during a visualization, have heavy limbs, or begin yawning. If this happens to you, don't worry, it is a very common reaction.

If you are unsure as to which practice may benefit you most, try utilizing one day for the next week. You will then begin to notice which ones you feel more comfortable practicing or receive the most benefits from.

Remember, that relaxed breathing techniques and visualization are not practices that are meant to be cure-alls for your mental health issues. They are one part of many building blocks that are going to help you understand your own unique mental health experience. So continue keeping up the review of cognitive distortions and exposure therapy.

8.9 Other Behavioral Activities

There following are other forms of behavioral activities that can help you better organize and schedule your life, so your emotions can feel further regulated.

8.9.1 Successive Approximation

This is a catch-all term that summarizes the act of breaking up large tasks into small steps, making your goal or activity easier to accomplish.

If we are faced with a huge goal, it is easy to become overwhelmed by the sheer mass of the project. If you are looking to have your house re-done before you sell it, or have to write a 30,000-word report for work, taking a look at it through the eyes of it as a whole can often make most people want to quit. If you have mental health issues, it is even easier to become overwhelmed and panicked about the task.

If you are being faced down by a seemingly large task, begin by writing down smaller steps that will be required in order for you to complete it. For example, if you are remodeling a home, begin dividing up the work by room, or theme of the room, such as the bedroom, living space, and a bathroom. Focus on the details of that room before you move onto the next. Once this first step is completed, moving onto the next step. By completely this first step you will already feel more accomplished and confident about completing the project entirely.

Try applying this practice into other portions of life where you feel overwhelmed, such as at work, school, or when problem-solving.

8.9.2 Writing Self-Statements to Counteract Negative Thoughts

Learning to counteract these thoughts takes practice as any habit suggested in this book. If you find yourself being constantly plagued by negative thoughts, try writing down a counteractive positive thought. This is helpful if you do not have the time to write out a thought record that challenges the thought.

If you have the thought that you are useless, try writing down what you feel you are good at. Think about your job, your hobbies, your favorite subject at school. It may be difficult initially to accept these counteractive thoughts. But the more you choose to bring out the positive, the less likely you are to associate yourself with the negative ones, and eventually stop believing them altogether.

8.9.3 Visualize the Best Parts of Your Day

Often people who suffer from depression have a negative bias' in their mind that is practiced on the daily. A negative bias is when a person possesses the ability to only see the negative parts of a person, situation, or experience. Beginning a gratitude journal as a part of your mental health maintenance may be a good idea so you begin seeing the good parts of your life, rather than focusing on what you see as the bad ones. At the end of each day, try to write down the parts of your day that stood out as the most positive. It could something as simple as a person smiling at you, or coming into contact with a cute dog. No matter how many negative points your day may have been riddled with, once you begin to make new associations with yourself, you will begin to notice how the positive begins to stand out for you.

If you are so inclined to try, writing down ten things that you are thankful for each day before or after you practice your relaxed breathing. This will help you associate the positive sensations with positive thinking, as well as give you some time to reflect upon what is going well in your life. This practice is not meant to ignore what may be bothering you, but to help you recognize elements of your life in a balanced manner. Life is not always lollipops and rainbows, but that is okay. It is always within your control to turn the direction in which your mind goes to interpret events, whether it be externally or internally.

8.9.4 Steps to Help You Control Your Emotions

Emotional regulation is a difficult concept to grasp for many people. Emotional upsurges are often the catalysts that throw us off healthy habits, whether it be related to physical, spiritual, or mental health. Our emotions can trigger us to overeat, to yell at someone for hurting our feelings, to misinterpret events, to drink too much, and to sit on the couch all day instead of checking things off our to-do list. Severe mental health problems are of course far more complex, but in essence, they are extreme emotions at the furthest end of the spectrum, often trigger us in similar ways, throwing off the habits we work so hard to keep in place.

Cognitive-behavioral therapy, or CBT, is a form of psychotherapy that links together the synchronicity of emotions with thoughts and behavior. It teaches ways that you can observe all three of these in action, noting how they affect one another and then learning to react in a way that is more reasonable and controlled. These selective methods will be described in further detail in the next chapter.

For now, here are a few steps that can help you identify your emotions before you choose to respond, rather than react instantly to any external or internal stimuli that may be around you.

1. Take a Step Back, and Do Not React Right Away: Reacting right away to any emotional triggers may result in many negative outcomes. People do have the tendency to make us angry, sad, or just generally hurt, and usually, our knee jerk

reactions are not proportionate to what we feel has been done to us. We don't have time to assess their motivations, their mood, or what might be going on in their lives. If you feel yourself being triggered, try to consciously stop yourself by closing your eyes, and taking a deep breath. Continue to sit and breathe like this for around five minutes, allowing your muscles to intense, and your heart rate to drop. When you feel yourself calming down, affirm to yourself that this sensation is only temporary. Try to make a time for later when you want to respond, should the occurrence require an adequate response.

2. Find a Healthy Outlet: Since you have managed your emotion, you need to find a way to release it. It is very unhealthy to keep things bottled up, as they can lead to stress-related disorders, as well as the worsening of mental health issues. Call or hang out with someone, of whose opinion you trust. Seeing occurrences from another person's perspective does just that; it lends an unbiased, third party opinion. Perhaps, keep a journal that

is separate from your notebook, write down the emotions you feel when someone or something triggers you. Exercise is great for releasing negative energy; from running to kickboxing. Some people find it more helpful to meditate. Be honest with yourself, and find a way to release the energy that is pent up inside you and may cause you to react too quickly.

3. See the Bigger Picture: Instead of choosing to react at the moment, try to let yourself see the bigger picture of the occurrence; meaning, things that will connect to the seemingly negative occurrence later down the line. You won't be able to see it at the moment, especially if you are angry or upset, but once you have calmed down, try to remind yourself that there is more to life than possibly overreacting to this occurrence.

4. Replace your Thoughts: As will be explained later, negative emotions easily bind with negative thoughts, and continuously following down the path of negative thoughts will only lead to more negative thoughts. Instead of reacting instantly or

ruminating about an issue, once you have calmed down, imagine the ideal resolution to your problem playing out or something else that instantly makes you happy; like your pet, or perhaps your partner.

5. Forgive your Emotional Triggers: Everyone has individuals in their lives that have faster access to their emotional triggers; it may be a family member, a friend, a co-worker, etc., someone who knows just how to press your buttons, oftentimes without knowing it. Becoming instantly irritated by your friend, who always leaves a light on when they visit your place, or a parent who always bothers you about not working out enough, isn't abnormal. If you feel these things for people you are close to, or even people you are not, do your best to forgive yourself for feeling these things. You are a human being, and it is entirely normal to feel this way sometimes. When you forgive, you detach. You detach from resentment, the jealousy, or anger rising inside you. Do not add to your mix of emotions by being angry at yourself.

As a practice exercise, perhaps you can write down a list of the top 10 things that instantly agitate or upset you. It can anything as large as the examples previously mentioned, such as the habits of others that bother you, or even an emotional reaction to people on the internet. Rank these emotions from 1-5, 5 being the most intense and harder to resist, 1 being the least intense and easier to resist. Start with the lowest number, and go through the previous steps. It will not be a concrete series of steps, as opposed to steps that will increase your awareness. Once you practice them, they will become easier and easier to recall without reading this section of the book. And once you recall them, it will easily form into a new and healthy habit.

Chapter 9: Increasing Your Power to Influence People

Once you are able to get a firm grip on your emotions, it'll be easier to learn about new ways that you can influence others in order to attain what it is you want out of life. This doesn't mean that you will manipulate people; manipulation requires a high level of deception. Influencing people is the art of getting your message properly across to people, so you can completely benefit from their understanding. Like everything written in this book, it takes practice, as well as consistent application. It also of course matters in what aspect of your life that you want to apply this. This section will mostly focus on work/career influence in positions of leadership.

Forbes lists 5 ways that you begin harnessing this ability of leadership and influence, as well as five categories of styles of influence. The styles are listed as follows:

1. Asserting: You insist that your ideas need to be heard and you challenge the ideas of other people.

2. Convincing: You put forward your ideas and offer further logical, rational reasons to convince others of your point of view.

3. Negotiating: Searching for compromises to make confessions and to reach outcomes that satisfy your greater goals and interests.

4. Bridging: You build relationships and connect with others by listening, and building friend groups and coalitions.

5. Inspiring: You express your opinion and position by encouraging others with a shared sense of purpose and unique possibilities.

All of these styles can just as effective, depending upon what kind of audience you are using it on. Do not fall for the 'one-size-fits-all' approach, because it will not work. Every situation and audience of whom you are trying to influence is going to be very different.

Here are the five steps that will help you increase your influence over others:

1. Find and understand your Influencing Style: This is once more all about self-awareness. What is your dominant style of the above? Try to observe yourself at work, or even when you are out with

friends, which category you feel you fall into. Try to understand your natural inclination so you can use it to start influencing others before you try adopting other styles.

2. Take Stock of Your Situation: Think of the individuals that you have to win over in your given situation in order to gain what it is that you want. What influencing style might affect them the most? If you are in an emergency situation, being assertive would definitely be the style to go for. If you need to win over someone over a longer period of time, you would more than likely choose to bridge.

3. Identify your Gaps: No one is good at everything, there are definitely certain aspects of the styles listed above that you may not be the best at applying. Find out where you are flawless and where your gaps lie, so you can effectively switch styles, given each satiation that presents itself to you.

4. Develop: Once you have found your gaps, you can find ways to develop your skills within those areas. This could be through a workshop, or by asking someone of whom you feel is particularly good at this influencing style to teach you. You

can role-play with them, so you can practice and gain confidence.

5. Practice: Begin with the small steps, low-stake situations that will not result in much negativity should you mess it up. Target a person where you would like to receive a certain outcome, and practice a certain influencing style. See what works, and what doesn't. Make note of this mentally so you can move forward into situations where the results are more high-staked.

The practice is truly the key to forming most habits. Make the time in your notebook and prioritize what you read in this book, and you will begin to see that you are merely participating in these actions naturally.

Chapter 10: Overcoming Anxiety, Panic Attacks, Depression, Stress and General Worries

As previously mentioned, Cognitive Behavioral Therapy is a certain kind of treatment that is used for people who suffer from depression, anxiety, anger issues, and panic attacks. The following section will zone in on the particular techniques that the therapy utilizes in order to help those suffering from the various issues that get in the way of their healthy habits. While this section is going to focus more on those with more severe mental health issues, there are still techniques and strategies that can help the general worrier or person who less often succumbs to a depressive episode.

If you feel you are suffering from depression, anxiety, anger issues, panic attacks, or any of the mental health issues mentioned in this book, it would be best to consult for a mental health professional while taking part in these strategies. They would work best as a guide as you forward and take charge of your emotions do your best to instill new habits of mental self-care.

10.1 Noticing your Cognitive Distortions

It is going to take time and practice for you to get into the pattern of noticing when you are applying some of the cognitive distortions previously mentioned. Like any muscle, it needs to be exercised, trained, and flex. Before long what initially took hours of note-writing will turn into a new, automatic way of thinking that happens inside of your mind within seconds. The neural pathways in your brain have been so used to going in one direction, that the sudden desire to turn them the opposing way will surely cause some discomfort, emotionally and mentally. Give yourself some time, and don't be so hard on yourself. It took this amount of time for the cognitive distortions to build themselves into your experience of depression, anxiety, and anger, so it will take time for it to grow into more adaptive reactions. Habits take time to form, and there is no limit on the space of time necessary in order to execute change.

Try to bring your notebook with you wherever you go, or make a document on your phone where you can try noticing some of these cognitive distortions. Pay attention to what you say to yourself and what kind of emotions accompany these thoughts. As previously stated, you have already made note of the cognitive distortions that you feel are bothering you most. If you are having difficulty identifying them, this section will list the most common amongst those that experience anxiety, depression, and anger issues.

10.2 Cognitive Restructuring: A Practice

Cognitive restructuring is a useful technique and strategy that helps you understand the underlying meanings behind your mood, thoughts, and behaviors. It is a life-long practice that challenges some of your most common cognitive distortions, sometimes called 'automatic thoughts/beliefs,' It can help you change the negative thinking that lies behind the experience of a down, angry, or anxious mood.

There are seven steps that you can apply while within the moment of experiencing a negative mood, such as anxiety, depression, and anger. These steps will be described and are meant to help your situational, along with deep breathing and relaxation exercises. We will later explore other thought-record/challenging exercise through similar charts like the ones you used to observe your thoughts and moods.

Here, I will use the specific example of a person with generalized anxiety, who feels triggered by having to eat in a public place. They are beginning to feel a panic attack coming on, and thoughts are racing through their head. *MindTools.com* suggests the application of the seven steps:

Calm Yourself: Deep breathing and meditation practices will be described in a later chapter that will help you feel better in the moment when a negative mood is triggered.

Identify the situation: Describe the situation that triggered your negative mood. In this case, it was the abrupt realization that the person needs to eat lunch with coworkers or a friend unexpectedly.

Analyze your Mood: Identify how you are feeling, and be honest about it. Moods are distinguishable from thoughts because they usually involve a single word. In this example, one word would be easy to identify; anxiety.

Identify Automatic Thoughts: Try to notice the automatic thoughts that are rising in your mind as your mood begins to come about. Some examples in this situation might revolve around the fear of judgment, the fear of having someone notice your anxiety, the fear of a panic attack, etc.

Find Objective Support Evidence: Find evidence that supports your automatic thoughts. Look at it objectively, without emotion. In this situation, a person may use examples of why the person may judge them, or that their eyes moved down to their shaky hands, etc. It would be important not to dwell on what we are assuming the other person is thinking of you because there exist no objective facts that say just that.

Find Objective Contradictory Evidence: When you arrive upon a balanced view, which is defined as seeing a situation as objectively as possible, which is what it means to gather facts about a situation. This is meant to instill the notion that thoughts nor are emotions facts. In this example, the balanced thought may sound something like; "they may notice my anxiety, but that's okay," or "there is no evidence that tells me that they have noticed my anxiety, nor has it shown that they will disapprove of it." These replaced thoughts are meant to calm you down and bring you to a more even state.

10.3 Restructuring Depression

Challenging thoughts as it relates to depressive symptoms is very similar to that of a person with anxiety. Thoughts are believed to be an incredibly powerful influencer for those who have suffered from depression for a long time. Very often, a person is so deep and set in their ways of feeling depressed, their behavior coordinates along with their thoughts, which only furthers the cycle of their negative mood. CBT attempts to infiltrate this cycle by asking the sufferer to observe their thoughts and realize that they are not as realistic as their accompanying emotions believe them to be.

The previously mentioned thought record is recommended for the use of those who are depressed as well. It looks at feelings, physical sensations, behaviors, and thoughts as they work together in a single experience of depression. Another example will be explained here as it relates to an individual with depression as opposed to someone with anxiety.

Since you have previously observed your mood, you more than likely have noticed common themes in what will trigger a more downward mood or time of day, or whether or not you had taken medication, exercised, etc. For some people, their depression is worse in the morning, a low mood is triggered by an argument, or in relation to work, or ruminating about a past relationship. These are only a few examples.

It may be harder for someone who has been stuck in a depressive state for a long time to take note of when their mood is at its worst vs when it is not as bad. This is why it is important to follow through on the first steps of this book, that focuses entirely on the observation of mood.

In this example, I will use the example of job seeking. is a very common trigger for many people suffering from depression. Perhaps they were just let go, or are having a difficult time finding work. First, you will write the date and time. Next, you describe the situation. In this case, it could be the mere fact that you have not heard back from any jobs that you applied to, or just received an email that rejected you from a certain role. This may cause you to feel depressed. In this section, describe the physical sensations you feel that accompany these automatic thoughts. Some people feel a drop in their stomach, tear-eyed, nausea, weak limbs, or the desire to lie down and not move all day. Some automatic thoughts that may arise are:

"I am never going to get a job."

"No one wants to hire me because I'm useless."

"I've wasted my life and have amounted to nothing."

In the next section, you will describe the emotions the best way you can that accompanied the thoughts. The descriptions can be as general as sad, mad and frustrated. If you feel the need to go into more detail than feel free to do so. Rate the emotions in intensity from 0-100.

Now, take a look back in your notebook at the cognitive distortions you identified as being your most common go-to's. In this example, the person is experiencing all-or-nothing thinking, overgeneralization, and catastrophizing. Write down the styles you feel your thoughts are reflecting in this section of the table. Then, ask yourself the questions that are written at the bottom of the table. This asks you to search for evidence that each thought is true, and then untrue. You may need extra paper for this section. Do this for each thought? In this example, evidence searching could appear as follows, as well as a rating from 0-100 on how much you actually believe the thought:

Thought 1: "I am never going to get a job":

Evidence of truth: None.

Evidence of Lies: I cannot predict the future. I have also had jobs in the past, so this statement just isn't fact.

Thought 2: "No one wants to hire me because I'm useless."

Evidence of truth: Email received from employer applied to.

Evidence of Lies: 'No one' is a very sweeping statement. I have not met everyone in the world who is hiring someone. No one has ever called me useless before.

Thought 3: "I've wanted my life and have amounted to nothing."

Evidence of Truth: Do not have a lot of savings, still live at home, do not have a partner.

Evidence of Lies: My life is not over yet. I am only X age. I have a roof over my head. I have held jobs in the past and have been successful and thrived in them.

Now, in the final column, you will re-assess your automatic thoughts and gauge how much you actually believe these statements that you have made, using the same rating system. Observe your emotions and rate their level of intensity.

Try to apply this automatic thought record response to your top five most mistaken beliefs that contribute to your depression. Link them once again to cognitive distortions, and go over this workout in relation to each of them. This may be something that is more difficult to do, depending upon the intensity of your depression.

Goal-seeking for those with depression is also highly important for recovery and will be discussed in a later chapter. For now, try to write out an automatic thought record once a day this week, or once every other day.

Discuss it with your partner, or someone you trust if it feels overwhelming.

10.4 The ABCDE Model of Cognitive Restructuring

The above model is an example of how events, behaviors, emotions, and beliefs all work together in conjunction and allow a certain mental health issue to thrive. Recognizing the link between them has been proven to help those suffering from depression. This form of restructuring can be recalled as:

A= Activating Event: An event that leads to the thoughts that led to emotional or behavioral issues.

B= Belief or thought about the event.

C= Consequences: Behaviors and feelings that come out due to the thoughts about the activating event.)

D= Deciphering: Recognizing and understanding, then finally defeating automatic negative thoughts.

E= Evidenced based positive thought development.

The ABCDE Model can also be used as a thought record for those with depression. Each letter would represent a single column that describes the particular event, the reaction to the event, and the re-framing that occurring to begin looking differently at the event. It can be presented as follows:

- A: Situation, thought, or physical sensation; do your best to be specific. Describe the 'who, what, where, when.' With an example of a person with depression, the activating event may be the thought like: "I am not attractive enough to find a partner." This thought could have been triggered by rejection, or a perceived reject, or even come out of the nowhere once the discussion or thought of dating arose around them.

- B: Listing all of the thoughts you had about A; then describe which thought caused the most depressing feeling. Then rate how true you think this thought is. For example, a thought that may accompany the triggering event A (which is also thought; thoughts can be triggering events too); maybe "yeah, I'll probably just end up dying alone.' From a rating from 1-10, this may have caused this person the intensity of depression at a 9.

- C: This section describes the accompanying actions and feelings. Describe specifically how you feel. Identify which feels directly tied to your activating event (A). Rate how strong that feeling is again on a scale of 1-10. Then write down the behaviors/reactions you made to your activating event. Then try to observe and see which behavior is most associated with the activating event. In our example, it may read as follows; "I feel like a complete loser. I feel ugly and unwanted. This feeling is at the intensity of an 8. I was lying in bed and swiping on tinder and decided to delete the app entirely. I tried to sleep but ended up crying for a while."

- D: Try to find which thought caused the most depressed and unpleasant feeling. Locate the cognitive distortion this thought falls under. Note if the thought is true if it is a productive way you think, what others may think about your thoughts and reaction. Access if your behaviors are rational. Explore yourself and question if you would be having this thought if you weren't distressed? An example of a reply to this section would be: "The thought that bothers me to the most is the one that predicts that I will 'die alone'. This is an overgeneralization. The thought isn't necessarily true because my life is not over yet. This does not help me feel better about myself. An observer may think that I am too hard on myself and says that dating comes in phases of life. My action of deleting the app is not rational because it may help me actually meet someone when I am ready. If I wasn't so stressed about being single, I probably wouldn't be having this thought."

- E: The final section applies what cognitive behavior therapy is mainly known for; the search for evidence that supports, and evidence that does not support mistaken beliefs and thoughts. It asks for you to replace the most powerful negative thought with a more rational, healthy thought. If you have control over the issue, try to think of proactive ways you can make yourself feel better. It is recommended that you do guide breathing or relaxation exercise (which will be discussed later). Finally, evaluate how you are feeling, between 1-10, and your thoughts, between 1-10, depending on how rational they are. Our example may state: "A thought that is more positive to replace the thought of 'I am just going to die alone' is 'Maybe I will find someone who best suits me one day, but it is okay if I don't too.' Actions I could take would be ones that invest me in my own hobbies rather than into someone else. If I wanted to date I can try to go out more often, or let my friends know that I am open to dating. I re-evaluated my feelings on the intensity and they are at a 5; the level of rationality has also gone down to a 5."

Thought records and cognitive restructuring such as the one mentioned above are not meant to permanently rid you of thoughts that bother you. They are merely meant as a practice to help you re-learn how to think and behave in healthier, and beneficial ways. Not all thought records will work for everyone, so feel free to try a few of them. No, not to be hard on yourself should your depressive mood not instantly live. It is not meant to instantly. It will be constantly emphasized in this book how important practice as, like any sport, it takes time to be mastered.

10.5 Coping with Physical and Psychological Sensations During Exposure: Fear of "Losing Control"

One of the hardest parts of exposure therapy is that it involves intentionally causing anxiety. The majority of the time, the ways in which people cope with their anxiety is to avoid it altogether. The initial experience of putting yourself into an anxiety-inducing situation will feel like the worst anxiety you have ever felt. There are the physical sensations of anxiety; the shaking, the racing pulse, the sweating, take make you feel like you cannot focus and convince you that you are not in control. This mix in with psychological sensations, such as thoughts that accompany the feeling of fear. Some accompanying thoughts might include the fear of going crazy, losing control, and the basic assumption that you will not be able to cope with the feelings you are having.

The entire point of ERP is to allow you to learn that these thoughts are not true. That goes along with the previously identified cognitive distortions you noted in the previous chapter. In order to learn to cope with the associated physical and psychological sensations during exposure, you must make sure you are making a hierarchy that is reasonable, and are doing it on a daily basis. If you are seeing a therapist, you can possibly begin doing it with them. Or you can do it with a person you trust. If the concept of putting yourself in vivo (meaning 'live' or 'in-person') exposure, you can begin with your first step via imagined exposure. The process is still the same, and you must do your best to allow the anxiety to fall from its increased state to a 30 or 0 before stopping the exposure.

Interceptive exposure is yet another form of exposure therapy that is mostly meant for those who suffer from anxiety disorders, panic disorder, and post-traumatic stress. It focuses mainly on how one can cope with the physical sensations that come with the experience of a panic attack. It has also been used as a method to stimulate anxiety in those with social phobia, generalized anxiety disorder, or those who have panic disorder with an accompanying medical condition.

10.5.1 In Panic Disorder

This form of exposure therapy intentionally causes anxiety and the physical sensations that come with it. People with panic disorder often associate the experience of certain physical sensations of that of an oncoming panic attack. Their fear of these sensations, in turn, will more than likely cause them to have a panic attack.

Like exposure and response prevention, interceptive exposure is meant to show the individual that the experience of anxiety in a physical manner is just that; the experience of something uncomfortable, rather than that of something that indicates doom.

Therefore, exposure exercise for the person with panic disorder will include many physical activities that stimulate a similar physical response that a supposed oncoming panic attack does. If you suffer from panic disorder, try participating in these exercises. Once again, try to rate the level of anxiety you feel next to the suggestion. Once you participate in one, observe yourself, and realize that the sensations are the result of actual physical exertion. They are always sensations that you can learn to cope with, not indicators of a bigger problem:

- Run on the spot for 30 seconds to 1 minute (will cause a racing heart, chest discomfort).

- Run up and downstairs for 30 seconds to 1 minute (will cause racing heart, chest discomfort).

- Shake your head from side to side, or move the head around by drawing a circle around you with your nose for 30 seconds (dizziness will be triggered).

- Spinning around in place for 30 seconds (dizziness and nausea may be caused).

- Stare at your hand for 2 to 3 minutes (feelings of unease, things looking 'weird' sensation).

- Wear a tight turtleneck or scarf around your neck for a few minutes (will create choking sensations).

- Tense as many muscles in your body as you can for 1 minute (can create muscle stiffness and soreness).

If you are planning on undertaking these exposures, include someone in their planning, like a close friend or parent. Try to engage in at least one day. Once you have physically induced similar anxiety-like physical sensations, observe your automatic thoughts that long to control your sensations. Often the fear of a heart attack or death will arise in you if you have been suffering from panic disorder for a long time. Instead of following those thoughts and trying to control the sensation, choose to notice the sensation, and do nothing to control it. Write down next to the activity how you felt when you chose not to control the sensation.

Once you begin to make it a habit of exposing yourself to these sensations, you will begin to create a new association between the normal experience of them and your mind; one that is indifferent and more realistic.

10.5.2 In PTSD

Post-traumatic stress disorder is an anxiety disorder that associates the sensation of physical symptoms with a previously experienced trauma. Similar suggestions to those that were made for the person with panic disorder will be made for those with PTSD. People with this disorder fear the experience of their physical symptoms as it relates to their particular trauma. They are often overly sensitive to anything that causes physical arousal, such as loud sounds, or even people yelling. The exposure will be very specific to the person's experienced trauma and will be drawn out in a systematic manner, in a safe place with a person the individual feels safe with around. Other forms of therapy along with CBT are important in the treatment of PTSD and should be undergone with the presence of a therapist.

10.5.3 In Social Phobia

The experience of social anxiety disorder or social phobia is greatly associated with the experience of the physical symptoms that accompany anxiety. A person with social anxiety not only fears the particular situation but also the possibility that the expression of their anxiety might be seen by others and cause them to be embarrassed. Many people fear that they may be seen shaking, sweating, stuttering, fiddling, or breathing heavily. So there are two sides to this form of anxiety that go hand-in-hand. Interceptive exposure aims to once again, help you learn that you can experience anxiety symptoms and that you can indeed cope with them in a social situation. Some suggestions for this form of exposure would be to induce sweating before a social engagement, or going to the store after having too much caffeine to induce shaking. This shows you that even if anxiety symptoms are present, it does not necessarily mean that people are going to notice them. It also means that you are more than capable of coping with the symptoms.

10.5.4 In Generalized Anxiety

People with generalized anxiety disorder have general worries about life, death, finances, relationships, children, travel, etc. The form of interoceptive exposure therapy that would be applied depends upon some of the main themes of anxiety you may possess. A therapist may ask you to drink coffee to induce racing thoughts, to show you that you can cope with the physical sensations of anxiety.

The entire point of this form of exposure therapy is to separate the cognitive association many people with anxiety disorders have with the experience of physical sensations. The experience of physical sensations is secondary forms of anxiety that pile upon the already large pile of triggers most people with anxiety disorders may have. But it is very important for you to engage in this form of therapy with another person around, along with the approval of your medical doctor.

Some people may have other physical conditions that would render this form of therapy less useful.

If you do choose to engage in this form of therapy, download and use this worksheet as a reference so you can note down how you feel in response to each event of exposure (from *www.psychologytools.com/download-therapy-worksheets/*)

10.5.5 Imagined Exposure

Imagined Exposure is a similar form of exposure therapy, but is taking place in the person's mind as an exercise rather than in the situation (commonly referred to as 'in vivo' exposure). There are many forms of imagined exposure exercises that can help many people who suffer from anxiety, depression, and anger issues.

10.5.6 With Anxiety

The process undergone to participate in this form of exposure is very similar to that of in vivo exposure:

Create a hierarchy of fears. Rate them in order of most feared.

Begin with the least anxiety-inducing fear.

Expose oneself to the anxiety-inducing fear.

Monitor the experience of anxiety

In imagined exposure, it is important to construct the scene of fear as vividly as possible. For this example, we will use a person who suffers from social phobia. Perhaps a fear that is lower on their hierarchy is going to the gym. Their fear has been divided up into 4 or 5 steps that they feel is required to get them inside the gym and to eventually exercise in public. The first step is to simply step inside the gym doors. Imagined exposure is best conducted with another person, or therapist, who can detail the experience while the client sits with their eyes closed and projects the experience in their mind. The therapist describes the experience as vividly as possible; sounds, smells, touches, possible interactions. The client is asked how they are feeling through the imagined scene. Sometimes the imagined exposure is recorded so the client can take it home and listen to the imagined exposure over and over again. Numbers are used to recording experiences of anxiety and progress down the line like that of exposure that will occur in person.

Imagined exposure is commonly used in conjunction with other forms of therapies for those with PTSD. In vivo exposure is often most feasible for people who have experienced trauma such as car accidents, physical or sexual abuse, or the observation of a violent event. Imagined exposure allows the individual to bring themselves back into the fear of trauma and to re-construct their beliefs surrounding the incident.

10.5.7 In Vivo Exposure

'In vivo' is an expression used in CBT therapy that refers to 'in the moment' exposure. It is the direct opposite of imagined exposure. Imagined exposure is often used before in vivo, especially if an individual is very fearful or resistant to committing to exposure. In vivo exposure is direct conformation with the feared object or experience.

10.5.8 Social Anxiety Disorder

In vivo exposure will involve many of the same steps that exposure and response prevention for OCD did. First, make a list of situations that make you the most anxious. Start with the least anxiety-provoking, and rate the level of anxiety you may feel on a scale of 0-100. Your list might look something like this:

Walking past a big group of people: 40-50

Saying hello to my coworkers: 50-60

Using my debit card at the store: 70-90

Using public transit: 90-100

Speaking in front of a group: 100

Begin with the lowest level of anxiety that you believe you may feel while in that situation. In this case, it would be number 1, walking past a big group of people.

If the concept of doing this is too anxiety-provoking, try to break down the exposure into steps. In this example, it may involve slowly starting to walk by larger groups of people, or increasing the proximity in which you are walking near others. Your exposure breakdown may look something like this:

- Walk past two people at X distance.

- Walk past two people at a closer distance.

- Walk past three people at X distance.

- Walk past three people at a closer distance.

You could increase the number of people, to the point where it grows into an undefined amount of people, at which point it will not matter because you have learned that you are able to cope with your anxiety.

Your anxiety will only lower once you consistently participate in an exposure. The point of exposure is to feel the anxiety, and allow it to lower, which in psychology is called habituation. You will become adjusted to the experience because you have decided to no longer flee the situation.

For each exposure, write down the level of anxiety felt, and wait for the SUDS level to lower to a 30. Once the anxiety has gone down to a zero, you can move onto your next anxiety-provoking situation.

10.6 Generalized Anxiety Disorder

Once again, you will be asked to make a hierarchal list of your most anxiety-producing stations or triggers. For a person with generalized anxiety, the trigger could literally be anything. If you are able to identify themes within your anxiety, write them down, and then write associated anxieties that circle around them.

For example:

- Death: Death is a common theme amongst those with generalized anxiety. This person may also have panic disorder, which furthers the anxious theme that focuses on their own possible death. The person may also fear the death of their family members loved ones or even strangers. Unlike OCD, the person does not participate in rituals, instead, simply ruminates over the possibility of something horrible occurring.

- Financial Loss: Many people worry about their career, how much money they have, how much money they will have, whether or not they will be able to provide for their children, etc. This leads to obsessive worrying without any proactive solutions.

- Relationship Loss: A person may constantly worry that they are not enough for their partner in a relationship. They worry about them leaving them, finding someone else, finding things they don't like about them, etc.

If you are able to come up with these themes, or any other kind, write them down, along with the thoughts that accompany them.

In vivo exposure for generalized anxiety disorder is dependent about whether or not the exposure is feasible. For example, if you have a fear of death, a therapist may suggest that you go for walks in a cemetery, or to participate in activities that directly trigger the thoughts about death. Make a list of the things that make you most anxious, rate them between 0-100. It will depend upon your specific theme of anxiety as to what you will expose yourself to. But no matter what it is, it is very important that you begin small, work your way up, and not stop until the anxiety has lowered to 0 to each step.

Chapter 11: Becoming More Organized

Since you have become better scheduling, self-care, creating boundaries, and making your mental health a priority, it is time to start becoming a more organized person. Lacking organization goes hand-in-hand with scheduling, and both form a delicate balance of instilling new and healthy habits. Lacking organizational skills can be the underlying reasons for the breakup of relationships, job loss, and overall baseline of stress felt. You may feel extra stressed in the morning before work because you constantly lose your keys, or didn't make time the night before to make your lunch. This could theoretically, bring down your entire day, because you are already stressed before you get there, and thus, will not be as productive.

Here is a list of the various ways that you can become more organized so you rid yourself of the extra stress that you are feeling in your life. The following tips are more general and may overlap with the previously mentioned ways of helping you create new habits.

- Write Things Down: The human brain is not made to recall all information. There is only so much we can store in there. Try writing down important dates, grocery lists, ideas you may have for a creative project, and you will find that you start to remember them naturally without having to consult the sheet of paper.

- Making Schedules and Deadlines: This was already discussed in a previous chapter, but it is safe to emphasize now; if you want to be a productive person, you need to adopt the habit of scheduling yourself. This will, in turn, help you become more organized in your life. Creating deadlines for yourself will also help you feel more productive because you actually complimented something! This energy will carry you forward in a positive manner, onward into the next goal or task.

- Don't Procrastinate: This is, of course, a lot easier said than done. Learning not to procrastinate is a habit in itself. Putting the effort into getting things done at the time that you designated will only make you feel more confident about the next task at hand. You will feel less stress, and moving onto another goal will feel more compelling, rather than burdensome.

- Give Everything a Home: It is easy to misplace things if you do not have an area in which you consistently put something. If you make it a habit to put your car keys in a bowl on the kitchen counter every time you get home, then you are far less likely to lose them. Keeping your life organized means keeping your things in the places they belong to. People who are organized keep order by storing things in the spot they designated for them. If it is something you use often, keep it out and in front of you, not miscellaneous, but specified, such as pens and pencils in a cup.

- Declutter Regularly: If you are a messy person, this is a habit that you have formed. So it is going to be a bit harder to change that around. Begin by choosing one area of your house/apartment a week, and declutter it, finding a home for everything that is vital to you. Once you have finished organizing everything, try to keep up this weekly habit, so you do not fall back into the routine of clutter.

- Keep Only What You Need: More stuff means more mess. People who are organized only keep what they need and really want. Having fewer things will help you to feel less stressed, as well as having fewer things to have to clean. If you have a lot of things and have trouble with this, try to write down the things right off the top of your head that you feel you need and want. Then write a list of the things that you own. Compare them, and begin crossing off the things that you know you do not need.

- Stay Away from Bargains: Going for sales will make you more likely to buy things you do not need, just because they are on sale. Try to keep a list of the things you actually need, or really want. If you are going shopping, keep this list close by, but without money. Then once you return from your trip, check on that list and see if anything you say was on it. This will avoid the trap of impulse purchasing.

- Delegate Responsibilities: Being organized means you have less to do, and most of all, fewer things that you more stressed. If you are filled with responsibilities and things to do on your to-do list, try to re-prioritize, or give the task for someone else to do. Watch the stress fall away from you as your list of things that are your responsibility becomes smaller.

- Work Hard: If you want to stay organized, you are going to need to put in a lot of effort. As previously mentioned, changing your habits can take from three months to a year to completely change. Sticking with it is going to be difficult, so be ready to put your best organizational foot forward.

Conclusion: Keeping Up with Good Habits

Now since you have begun to instill various new and healthy habits into your life, it is time to do your best to maintain them. This may be a fragile and anxious time for you, because you are thinking back on times perhaps, when you weren't able to start exercising more often, to stop thinking negatively, to eat more greens, etc. But this is the moment where you must let go of the past in order to benefit from the future. There are probably several reasons as to why these habits did not stick, which made you feel discouraged and frustrated. So, please tell yourself this now: relapsing into old habits is completely normal! If you want to work out more often, but you fell back into watching Netflix every evening of your week, try not to feel discouraged. All you can do is notice the behavior, and assess what may have gone wrong in trying to instill it. This is the only way that you are going to successfully re-try and bring about a new and positive habit for yourself.

Here is some advice on how you can make your good habits stick, as well as ways you can access what may have gone wrong in the past:

1. Start Very Small: A lot of people tend to think too large when it comes to new habits, and thus easily let themselves down. You have to try to be realistic with yourself; if you haven't even gone to the gym, telling yourself that you are now going to go for 5 evenings a week isn't' reasonable. You are more than likely going to let yourself down, and thus, feel more discouraged. With any habitual behavior, you may want to blend into your life, start very small, and work your way up from there. Research has shown that willpower is like a muscle, and gets very tired the more you use it. If you start small, you will adjust to trying something new, and will thus, not be disappointed in yourself.

2. Get Hooked on Your Habit: It becomes harder to let go of a project once you have invested a lot of time within it. The longer you have practiced a habit, the less likely you want to break it. Put a visual marker on your calendar every time you have done something that you want to instill. This

reminder will motivate you to continue practicing your habit.

3. Have Clear Intentions: This is where you have to try to become more specific with what you want to achieve in your habits. Research has shown that you are much more likely if you follow through on things that are clear and concise. This means, that you have to decide when and where this new habitual behavior will take place. Writing it down in a scheduling book will help you not only remember but feel more attached to achieving it.

4. Celebrate Your Small Wins: Celebrating your progress is crucial for staying motivated. Every time you reward yourself for achieving a goal, you activate the area in the brain that warms up when rewarded. Chemicals such as dopamine and serotonin, positive emotions, are released and thus become more associated with these reward behaviors. So do your best to reward yourself, no matter how small the changes may be.

5. Design Your Environment: Your environment is going to drive your behavior. If you leave cookies out, you are going to eat them. There is nothing unusual about that! If you want to achieve certain

goals, you may need to alter what is around you. If you want to watch less TV, then put the TV in a room that is away from you while you do other tasks. If you want to read more, try putting a good book next to you in bed. Making undesired things less accessible and more desired things more possible.

6. Surround Yourself with Supports: Having the right people in your corner that will not enable your habits is very key to success. People are generally most like the five people they spend the most time with, so it is very important to observe their habits, and thus, make a decision about your own. You may need to find other support groups who share your mindset.

7. Pre-Commit to Your Habit: When you add another layer of accountability to your habits, you are more than likely to follow through. If you have told someone that you are going to write every day, then they are going to ask you about it. If you have made a deal with a friend to start exercising before work, then canceling on them gives you more consequences than actually going. This isn't meant to guilt you, but to give you that

extra push when participating in your habit may feel extra hard that day.

You are now ready to start your habit changing journey. If there are times when you are feeling especially unmotivated, try to talk it out with a friend or loved one of whom you know will not judge you. It took a long time to create negative habits, so it is going to take some time to turn them around. Remind yourself too, that the human brain is a spectacular organ that does react to consistent change and effort. You are capable of this change; science has proven it so.